SMALL AND SUCCESSFUL IN JAPAN

For Carol and Kieran.

Small and Successful in Japan

A Study of 30 British Firms in the World's
Most Competitive Market

DR SIMON COLLINSON
Institute for Japanese–European Technology Studies
University of Edinburgh

Avebury

Aldershot • Brookfield USA • Hong Kong • Singapore • Sydney

Published by
Avebury
Ashgate Publishing Limited
Gower House
Croft Road
Aldershot
Hants GU11 3HR
England

Ashgate Publishing Company
Old Post Road
Brookfield
Vermont 05036
USA

British Library Cataloguing in Publication Data

Collinson, Simon
    Small and successful in Japan: a study of 30 British firms
    in the world's most competitive market
    1. Business enterprises, Foreign – Japan 2. International
    business enterprises – Japan
    I. Title
    338.8'8941'052

    ISBN 1 85628 921 4

Library of Congress Catalog Card Number: 96-83831

Printed and bound by Athenaeum Press, Ltd.,
Gateshead, Tyne & Wear.

Contents

v

Figures and tables

Preface

The interviews, discussions and information-gathering that went into this book have taken me many times, and in more ways than one, from academia in Edinburgh to corporate Tokyo, and back.

I am indebted to many people for their help, advice and insights into Japan and the Japanese, and the challenges faced by British firms in Japan. First and foremost thanks must go to Dr. Martin Fransman, the Director and founder of the Institute for Japanese European Technology Studies (JETS), who introduced me to Japan some years ago and continues to be an unsurpassed guide.

Members of the Industrial Competitiveness Unit in the Department of Trade and Industry had the foresight to help sponsor the initial study and the insight to realise the importance of small British firms as exporters, entrepreneurs and world-class competitors.

In Japan many individuals and organisations, both British and Japanese, provided assistance. Amongst others I received support from the Ministry of International Trade and Industry (MITI) and the Japan External Trade Organisation (JETRO). But I owe particular thanks to Ian de Stains at the British Chamber of Commerce in Japan (BCCJ), to Adrian Jenkyns, Soli Sethna and others in SAMBI (the Small and Medium-Sized Business Initiative of the BCCJ), and to Steve Plater at the British Embassy in Japan (Commercial Section). All of whom provided the kinds of contacts and introductions without which good research is impossible in Japan. I am also indebted to all the managers, employees, government officials and other interviewees that gave up their precious time to talk at length to me.

Finally, on a personal note, none of this work, or the lengthy fieldtrips abroad, would have been either possible or worthwhile without the support of Carol, and more recently, Kieran, who arrived along the way.

1 Introduction

In the 1980s, before the 'high-yen' (*endaka*) recession began in Japan, a flood of books appeared on the management practices of Japanese companies and on the Japanese economy more generally. These varied considerably in their approach and in the degree to which they shed any new light on the country's economic successes. To some extent at that time a lack of detailed research and in-depth understanding combined with a somewhat faddish demand for things Japanese from Western managers. This led to an exaggerated view of the competitive threat posed by Japan, the superiority of its companies, and the unassailable nature of its domestic markets. In many ways a common Western perception of Japan stemmed from a widespread 'fear of the unknown' as regards the country and its people. The worst cases promoted over-blown, stereotypical views of Japan and the Japanese, both positive and negative, exacerbating the general lack of understanding and turning fears into phobias.

In recent years a number of more realistic texts have appeared, based on a more sober and balanced appraisal of the strengths and weaknesses of the Japanese economic system and Japanese companies, and a more measured understanding of the Japanese people. This new realism partly comes from the obvious cracks that have begun to appear in the country's polished image of efficiency and success.

Paradoxically, as the fashion for Japan has waned, better insights about the country are also now being gained through the growing number of Westerners with experience of living and working in Japan and doing business with Japanese firms abroad. Similarly, there has been a rise in the number of Japanese observers and writers who are beginning to better understand and communicate how and why Japan is different (although the imbalance with the UK is still surprising with around 55 thousand Japanese living in Britain and just 12 thousand British living as foreign residents in Japan).

This book draws on the insights of both these groups, but especially on the

1

knowledge and experience of British managers currently running foreign businesses in Japan. Its main aim is to shed light on a subject that has attracted a great deal of attention (and is the source of some of the above phobias) but has surprisingly been the focus of relatively little detailed research. How can a foreign company sell successfully to the Japanese? How can a foreign company establish a successful business in Japan?

As a target for investment and exports it has been recognised for a long time that Japan is different and Japan is difficult. The phenomenal imbalance in foreign direct investment (FDI) and trade attests to this. Its reputation as a tough market, sometimes as an entirely closed market, has been so well emphasised as to discourage many potential entrants. But the real reasons underlying the imbalance, the real constraints to market entry are still not well understood.

The clearest single message that comes from those that have a long experience of managing businesses in Japan is that the Japanese market needs long-term commitment. This is one of the main issues examined in this book. What makes the Japanese market require this extra commitment? What makes the Japanese market *deserve* extra commitment? And once you have made the decision to get into this market how do make a success of it? What should you expect? How (and how much) should you change and adapt your existing product or service or your management and marketing practices?

Most of what was known up until now is anecdotal, and tends to reflect on the successes, failures and experiences of large-firms, because this is seen as more newsworthy by the business media and politicians alike. This book is different first and foremost in that it is a book about British small-and-medium sized enterprises (SMEs) based in Japan and it spells out the lessons learnt by managers and entrepreneurs who have lived and worked in Japan and succeeded in establishing businesses in Japan. Any insights it contains come directly from their experience, compiled through case study interviews.

The 30 British SMEs researched for this book proved to be a rich source of untapped information that is arguably far more relevant for the average manager wanting to learn about Japan and the Japanese or contemplating setting up a business in Japan. Without the investment finance, consultancy support or the in-house specialist expertise to by-pass the many barriers to market entry in Japan SME managers have tackled these constraints head-on. They have had to adapt products, services, management practices and in most cases their personal approach to doing business, to succeed in Japan's tough domestic market under 'local rules'.

The British success stories in Japan included in this survey are not widely known about. Many of them are operating in industry sectors where Japanese superiority and/or Japan's impenetrable domestic market have been all-too readily accepted in the West. An SME manufacturer producing ink-jet printers for labelling on production lines, based in the UK but with a rapidly-expanding branch selling to manufacturing companies in Japan, competing at the frontier of technology against giants like Toshiba and Hitachi. Two engineering companies with locally-registered subsidiaries both selling precision measuring equipment to leading Japanese manufacturers, including car companies, where the quality and technical sophistication of the equipment is essential to the buyers' leading-edge productivity and product quality. A slot-machine games developer and manufacturer now selling successfully in Japan after a long, uphill struggle against coordinated local Japanese competition. All are examples from which the lessons in this book are taken.

As well as interviewing senior managers and engineers, both British and Japanese, in a total of 30 British SMEs based in Japan, a wide range of other interviews took place with Japanese buyer companies, consultants, distributors, business organisations and government agencies in the UK and Japan. The latter include the top organisations involved in promoting trade and foreign direct investment in Japan on both sides, such as the Japan External Trade Organisation (JETRO), the Ministry of Trade and Industry (MITI), FIND (the Foreign Investment in Japan Development Corporation), Keidanren, the Small Business Corporation, the DTI, the British Embassy in Japan, the British Chamber of Commerce in Japan (and what was its 'SAMBI', small business group) and many others.

From this survey come a number of insights on Japan and the Japanese, and lessons on how to succeed in doing business in Japan's domestic market, the tough spawning ground of some of the world's leading companies. This book attempts to convey these insights and lessons by recounting the experience of some British SMEs that have managed to adapt, compete and succeed in Japan. It is not a source book for the practical details on legal matters, taxation, registration and the like, which can be found elsewhere. Neither does it attempt, despite providing some relevant background material, to give a comprehensive account of the Japanese economy or the nature of Japanese companies, except where such details are relevant to explaining the business activities of the British SMEs surveyed. Other books are available giving general facts and figures on Japan, and describing specific sectors and markets. The aim here is to convey more tacit, qualitative knowledge from those with first-hand experience.

Overview

This book is divided into 5 chapters. This one will provide some background to the research survey of British SMEs in Japan on which the book is based. It

describes the types of companies that were included in this survey, who we talked
to and what questions were asked. Chapter 2 gives some contextual information
about Japan, in the form of a brief introduction to its economy, society and political
infrastructure and moving on in the second part of Chapter 2 to some of the current
changes affecting all aspects of Japanese life. These include the recent recession
and continuing revival, social change, political upheavals and economic restructuring at the corporate and national levels. All these influences, past, current and
anticipated have implications for the main issue with which this book is concerned: the opportunities and constraints facing foreign SMEs trying to enter the
Japanese market. The final section in Chapter 2 provides an overview of trade and
foreign direct investment flows into and out of Japan and profiles the mixture of
foreign firms that have established themselves there. It also asks what the basic
attraction is. Why do a range of firms maintain a permanent presence in Japan?

Chapter 3 begins with the same question and answers it by examining
specifically why the range of British SMEs covered by this survey chose to
establish businesses in Japan. Chapter 3 and Chapter 4 examine the core findings
of the study, beginning with a review of the main entry methods, their drawbacks
and advantages and some of the ways companies have financed their initial
investment in Japan. Chapter 3 also reviews how the survey firms were assisted
by the British and Japanese Governments who offer a range of trade promotion
initiatives in their respective efforts to redress the trade imbalance (some relevant
addresses are listed in the Appendix).

Chapter 4 looks at the main difficulties facing SMEs trying to enter the
Japanese market and provides case-study illustrations of how managers have
adapted to cope with these constraints. The second part of this chapter reviews the
benefits that managers and engineers, based in Japan and in the UK, have gained
from their exposure to the tough economic environment in Japan. Has the
experience brought about improvements in organisational efficiency, manufacturing performance, technical expertise, innovativeness, marketing skills or
overall profitability? Have they learnt lessons that can be applied in other
corporate divisions in the UK, or in other international markets? Or have they just
lost money and learnt nothing?

The concluding Chapter 5 will tie the background material and the survey
findings together, bringing the research up-to-date with the on-going changes in
Japan and examining some of the emerging opportunities and constraints for
British small and medium-sized firms who are considering taking the plunge into
Japan.

A survey of British SMEs in Japan

Background

In the last 10 years, since the 'Plaza Accord', the rapid appreciation of the Japanese Yen has masked a very significant rise in the volume and real value of imports into Japan. Between 1985 and 1991 the value, in US dollar terms, of Japan's imports *trebled*, from $40.2 to $120.3 billion. In the same period manufactured goods, as a proportion of total imports, increased from 30 percent to 50 percent (and reached 58 percent in 1995, valued at $94 billion). Imports continued to climb in real terms throughout the '*endaka*' or high-Yen recession and although Japan's merchandise trade surplus in 1994 hit a record high for the fourth year running, again currency movements hid a real decline in the surplus (trends associated with the 'J-curve' effect). Between July 1994 and July 1995 exports grew 10.3 percent and imports by an unprecedented 28.6 percent (imports from the European Union increased by 34.3 percent), narrowing the trade imbalance significantly.

These trends point to the growing opportunities that exist in Japan for foreign firms, including British SMEs. Significant social and economic changes in Japan underlie this growth in imports, including the marked increase in Japanese consumers' acceptance of imported products, and the need to cut costs in Japanese companies, through buying cheaper imports. The origins of this book go back to a time when these trends were foreseen by foreign managers working in Japan, but had not yet fully emerged. Opportunities certainly existed but the barriers to entry into the Japanese market were arguably more severe and the entry routes less well-worn and small firms in particular had difficulties establishing themselves and their products in Japan.

The most obvious outward signs of these problems, and the existence of real barriers to market entry in Japan, has been the imbalance of trade and foreign direct investment (FDI) between Japan and the rest of the world (Chapter 2 gives a range of illustrative statistics and sources for these data). This has been particularly acute between the UK and Japan. Japan has a ratio of outward to inward FDI of 14 to 1, compared to 1 to 1 in the UK and in the UK it has invested over 22 times the amount that the UK has invested in Japan. Britain imports from Japan around three times the amount (by value) it exports to Japan, and has done so for some time.

Until very recently, however, relatively little was known about the real constraints for foreign firms in Japan, outside the groups of practising managers who had experienced these first hand. This placed further emphasis on the competitive strengths of Japanese firms, as a source of the imbalance in trade and FDI. It also set the stage for the drawn-out and at times misguided political challenge from the USA for Japan to open its domestic markets. Misguided in the sense that (as this and other books show) the real barriers for foreign firms tend to be factors inherent in the economic infrastructure and business behaviour that are an integral part of Japan and largely (and increasingly) beyond the control of the most senior politicians, who have less influence at the local business level than Japanese bureaucrats.

These are some of the main background factors prompting this study of British SMEs in Japan and subsequently this book. Funding for the project came from the Industrial Competitiveness Unit of the UK Government's Department of Trade and Industry (DTI) and their areas of interest also provide something of a rationale for the research. The DTI had:

1.   A remit to redress the above imbalance of trade and FDI with Japan by boosting exports.

2.   A need for further research to sharpen up government assistance schemes for British firms selling to Japan and establishing themselves in Japan.

3.   Indications that there were opportunities for British SMEs but a gap in the general understanding of where opportunities were and what SMEs would need to do to exploit them.

4.   A specific interest in industrial and manufacturing activities, including product development, the provision of technical back-up services and the practice of technology transfer in interactions with Japan.

5.   A remit to improve the competitiveness of British industry, here through learning from Japan.

Why the focus on manufacturing? This is linked to the trade issue as a whole, through a number of reports in the early 1990s that tie Britain's international economic competitiveness to its manufacturing strengths. Britain has always been a trading nation. We consistently export around $1500-worth more of goods and services per head of population than the USA and $1050-worth more than Japan. Overall, manufacturing is the UK's 'key tradeable sector' and contributes about three times as much to exports as services - i.e. a one percent drop in earnings from manufacturing would need to be matched by a three percent increase in earnings from services (or 20 percent from financial services)(DTI, 1993). Moreover, Japan is the UK's second biggest export market outside Europe, after the USA. Hence the attention on boosting manufacturing exports to Japan.

Figures show in general that UK competitiveness has improved since 1979, following a long and steep decline stretching back to the beginning of this century. British manufacturing is now supposedly stronger than at any time over the past 30 years. But, Britain is still placed number 18 out of 24 OECD countries in terms of GDP per head (at purchasing power parity) in a list we once dominated.

This study and this book combined these key areas by focusing on industrially-based British SMEs in Japan rather than consumer or service businesses. Industrial activities represent over two-thirds of UK exports to Japan yet receive relatively little attention from analysts and writers, who have tended to examine the distribution and marketing problems related to selling consumer products in Japan. The aim in particular was to dispel the myth that Japan is a closed market or too tough for British firms to succeed and to show that there are substantial rewards for those that persevere.

In addition to the huge realised and potential domestic market in Japan for foreign firms we were interested in how exposure to the tough Japanese market might have improved the competitiveness of UK firms, and what lessons could be passed on to other companies. Key aspects of industrial 'performance' include productivity, output growth, relative unit labour costs, real returns on capital employed, and shares of world trade. A central foundation of industrial performance and national competitiveness is the macroeconomic climate within which companies evolve and operate, responding to the specific market constraints and emerging opportunities offered by their economic environment. Therefore, exposure to Japan's notoriously competitive economic environment is thought to lead to improved performance in companies exporting to and operating in Japan.

The findings from the study, described in this book support this view, and the lessons learnt by the firms examined can be found here (the original report, by this author, was sub-titled: '*The Revealed Competitiveness of British Firms Abroad*'). Adapting successfully to Japan's economic climate entails learning that strengthens an individual manager and individual firms. The sheer success of Japan's economy suggests there are more lessons to be learnt there than elsewhere.

Survey coverage

The material for this book was gathered over a series of fieldwork trips to Japan in 1993 and 1994, after a pilot study in late 1992. These focused on the main DTI-funded study of British SMEs in Japan. One visit, sponsored by the Great-Britain Sasakawa Foundation, specifically examined buyer-supplier links between Japanese firms and foreign firms in Japan. The following section describes the range of firms covered by the survey and the focus of the interviews.

One of the central aims of the study on which this book is based was to examine and understand the problems facing British SMEs in Japan that were involved in the types of economic activity that forced them to adapt to the Japanese market, consumers and competitors. Of most interest were those manufacturing in Japan (rare amongst SMEs abroad), or directly adapting products and services for the Japanese market. This meant avoiding not only large firms but also those only involved in direct selling, like representative offices, or involved only in providing financial services, for example, when compiling the survey sample. A further requirement was that all companies should have at least one full time representative in Japan and should have started operations (at least in terms of the existing company structure) in the last 10 years.

Given these self-imposed limitations there were probably around 180 British SMEs appropriate to the aims of this project out of the estimated 400 British firms in Japan, at the time the research was carried out (1993-1994). The survey covered 30 full company case-studies, collected by interviewing senior managers (Japanese and British) in Japan and, where necessary, at UK headquarters. The survey questions focused on the following issues, divided into 7 sections:

1.   Establishing a base in Japan: why do British SMEs do it and how do they do it?

2.   How are British businesses in Japan financed? What is their relationship with Japanese banks and UK banks?

3.   How much commitment is required for the Japanese operation from home base? What are companies' long-term aims in Japan?

4.   What are the main difficulties of establishing a base in Japan and operating in the Japanese market and how have SMEs overcome these?

5.   Are there benefits for British SMEs operating in Japan?
     How are these passed on to customers, suppliers and to other parts of the firm?

6.   What type and level of support have companies received from British government sources? What do they believe is available? What would they like to be made available? How does this compare with other EC nations?

7.   What type and level of support have companies received from Japanese government sources? What do they believe is available? What would they like to be made available?

As mentioned earlier a second study focused particularly on the nature of buyer-supplier links between a number of the case-study firms and their local Japanese customers and sub-contractors, adding detail to the original survey.

The main interviews were with the most senior managers or local representatives in Japan, plus engineers, marketing advisors and other decision-makers, based in Japan. Additional interviews were held with divisional managers responsible for Japanese or Asian operations at the UK headquarters and/or with the person responsible for the initial market-entry (in both cases this was often the managing director, because of the small size of the firm). Liaison personnel who travelled frequently between the UK and Japan, or who were temporarily on secondment in Japan, could make direct comparisons between UK business practices and those in Japan from a 'fresh' perspective and therefore also made valuable interviewees. Their views on Japan often contrasted those of managers who had been in Japan for a long period of time and incorporating both provided for a more balanced survey.

A range of meetings were also held with distribution and marketing companies in Japan, with government officials responsible for import legislation and promotion and with local 'experts' and consultants who had considerable experience advising foreign companies. Over 80 structured interviews were held in total and these have been supplemented by numerous discussions since the end of the research project to update the survey.

The names of the companies and the interviewees and much of the financial data on companies that was collected during this study have not been included in this book for a number of reasons. First and foremost, by promising anonymity to interviewees and their companies we gain a frank and true account of the difficulties managers have faced in building their operations in Japan. Critical discussions of head-office management, local Japanese personnel, government assistance mechanisms, the tactics of local competitors and the like would not be possible if comments could be linked to interviewees and/or their companies. Also, the assurance that confidentiality will be respected, tends to open doors to more sensitive information about product development plans, accepted company accounting 'conventions' and marketing strategies, for example, that give a fuller picture of how firms have adapted to succeed in Japan.

Sample profile

The sample covers a wide range of firms including KK and YK-registered firms (*Kabushiki Kaisha* are joint-stock companies, *Yugen Kaisha* are limited liability companies, both registered in Japan), subsidiaries and majority-owned joint-ventures, manufacturers, service-providers and sales offices. Some were tied closely to corporate headquarters in UK or manufacturing bases abroad, others were on their own.

A key variation across the sample was the customer base addressed by different firms. Many British companies (about a third of those examined) deal predominantly with other Western companies in Japan and therefore face a different set of difficulties to those dealing directly with the Japanese. Contrasts between the various case studies added to the main insights from the survey.

Figure 1.1 provides an overview of the 30 case studies. It shows each firm's broad sector of operations using a basic description of products or services (bracketed) combined with a coding of their main activities in Japan (explained in the key). These categories of activity also tend to denote the degree to which the firm has invested locally. Thus, 'M' firms will have established manufacturing activities in Japan, 'PD' firms will be engaged in some form of 'hands-on' product development locally (usually adapting imports), 'TS' indicates that the firm provides customers with technical support in addition to selling the product and so on. 'C' is slightly different in that it denotes firms that are involved in the construction industry in Japan (generally as consultants or architects), but the level of investment and 'hands-on' involvement is commensurate with their position in this scale. 'IE' is for companies involved in simpler forms of import-export activities and 'OS' is a catch-all for the remaining service operations. The scale is hierarchical in that firms engaged in manufacturing also tend to be involved in product development, technical services, import-export activities and so on and firms involved in product development also tend to offer technical services and are engaged in import-export operations.

Figure 1.1 also shows the sample firms' basic structure or status in Japan. Branch operations are truly 'foreign' entities while KK-firms are locally registered. KK firms in the second column are headquartered in the UK and are effectively corporate subsidiaries, compared to independent KK firms, listed in the third column. Thus, discounting the 'newcomers' category, the firms are grouped from left to right according to the degree to which they are controlled from the UK. An important point to note is that all these firms are known locally as 'foreign' to a greater or lesser degree, and are treated as such by Japanese companies and customers.

As regards size, 16 of the 30 companies have fewer than 20 employees based in Japan, including 4 of the 9 branches, 3 of the 10 UK-headquartered KK's, 5 of the 7 independent KK's and all three newcomers. 6 firms have less than 20 employees overall and so can be defined as 'micro' enterprises. 25 firms have less than 100 employees in Japan and 10 have less than 100 overall.

In 12 of the sample firms the senior representative or 'President' in Japan (usually the main case-study interviewee) was Japanese and in two of the

——————————————————————— Company status in Japan ———————————————————————

Branches with UK HQ (9)	KK/YK* with UK HQ (11)	Independent KK/YK* (7)	'Newcomers' (3)
M (industrial solvents)	M (kaolin/ paper)	TS (computers)	PD (car wheels)
M (precious metals)	M (power supplies)	C (architecture)	OS (financial services)
TS (fluids equipment)	'M' (printing)	C (architecture)	OS (marketing)
TS (chemicals)	PD (measuring instruments)	IE (building materials)	
TS (electrical systems)	PD (measuring instruments)	IE (drinks)	
C (consultants)	PD (slot machines)		
C (consultant/contractor)	PD (photographic equipment)	OS (marketing)	
IE (computers)	PD (fluids equipment)	OS (interior design)	
OS (consultants)	TS (industrial printers)		
	TS (couplings)		
	TS (industrial pumps)		

decreasing amount of local investment (see key below)   ——————————————————————————> increasing amount of local autonomy

Characteristic activities of the 30 case-study SMEs in Japan (grouped to show a decreasing level of local investment 1-6):

    (1) M = manufacturing   (4) C = construction industry-related
    (2) PD = product development   (5) IE = import-export
    (3) TS = technical services   (6) OS = other services

* KK is *Kabushiki Kaisha* (joint stock company) and YK is *Yugen Kaisha* (limited liability company), both indicating that the firm is also registered as a company in Japan

(The firms' main products, services or industry sector are described in the brackets)

Figure 1.1   The main characteristics of the sample firms

remaining firms there were plans to hire a Japanese for the most senior management position as soon as a suitable candidate was found. The majority of sample firms in column two (the KK's with UK HQs) and over half of those in column one had Japanese Presidents and were run along Japanese lines. A useful contrast was between these and the independent KK firms (column three) which tended to be small enterprises run by British owner-managers many of whom had long-term experience in Japan.

A further contrast, in terms of local knowledge and problems experienced, was between the three newcomers and the other companies. The newcomers were all entirely British-run operations, with senior managers that were relatively new to Japan, while the others tended to be run either by British 'old hands' or Japanese representatives.

Before looking at the experiences of these firms, the difficulties they encountered and how they have adapted to succeed in Japan, it is necessary to provide some background on Japan and the Japanese, and this will be done in Chapter 2.

2 Japan: Past, present and future

To understand why Japan is different and why it is difficult compared to other foreign markets we need to understand something of its economic and social infrastructure, the country, its people and aspects of its past that have played a formative role in its post-war economic development. For some managers interested in the quick-fix lessons for success in Japan this may seem slightly irrelevant. But the message from those who have tried and eventually succeeded in Japan is that one of the major barriers to increased business with and in Japan *is our own lack of understanding about the fundamental differences between Westerners and Japanese*. The following background material provides some of the reasons why Japanese businessmen and Japanese companies interact and operate differently, with each other and with foreigners.

We also need to separate some of the myths about Japan from the current reality. How has the country grown so rich, so quickly, and will it continue to grow? What factors underlie this economic success story and how are they changing? Which of the 'classic' management tips for success in Japan are no longer valid?

This chapter focuses on the Japanese economy, companies and business behaviour but also touches on aspects of culture, religion and society that cannot be divorced from its economic characteristics and provides a general background for the later discussion of British firms operating in Japan. It will also look at the significant changes now taking place across all these dimensions, from the recent economic recession, changes in Japanese society and the continuing political confusion, to Japan's evolving role in the international arena.

Finally, before moving on to describe some of the findings from the UK SME survey in Chapters 3 and 4, there will be a brief overview of the current trends in trade and foreign direct investment between Japan and other OECD nations. Again this provides a context for the later case-studies.

The Japanese economy

Japan's Gross Domestic Product (GDP), over US$3,400 billion, makes it the second largest economy in the world after the USA. Its GDP per capita, at just over US$27,000, makes it one of the richest countries in the world, ahead of the USA (about US$23,000) and second only to smaller economies like Switzerland and the United Arab Emirates (Morimoto, 1995). This combination of size and wealth is related to the strength of Japan in the global economy and the importance of its domestic market for multinational companies of all sizes.

Between 1913 and 1950 Japanese GDP grew at an average annual rate of less than 1 percent alongside all the other current OECD member countries. Between 1950 and 1973 it grew at an unparalleled rate of 8 percent, over three times the growth rates of the UK and the USA in this period. Since 1973 until recently its average rate of growth has remained at three percent per year, double the UK rate and almost three times the US rate. The OECD itself noted this by observing: 'by the conventional measures of economic performance (income growth, inflation, unemployment) Japan has out-performed all other OECD economies since entry into the organisation in 1964'. How did this happen?

An important point to note to begin with is that the rapid development of Japanese industry during this time was characterised by key strengths in specific, strategic sectors, not across the board. It evolved from iron and steel and heavy engineering to cars and consumer electronics. A large and successful iron and steel industry, initially dominated by the New Japan Steel corporation, provided the foundation for shipbuilding in the 1960s and 1970s and the growth of giant heavy engineering groups (the pre-war 'zaibatsu'), like Hitachi, Kawasaki and Mitsubishi which later diversified into giant conglomerates. As the economy shifted from a reliance on textiles and primary metals to machinery, transport equipment and electrical equipment, so the structure of industry moved from being labour-intensive to capital-intensive.

Japan became the major global producer of passenger cars, producing almost 10 million at the beginning of this decade (almost double the US production, which has recently overtaken Japan once again) and exporting just under half. Again the sector was dominated by large companies, with Toyota manufacturing 30 percent of Japan's total output and Nissan producing 17 percent. It also developed very strong electronics and consumer electronics sectors initially based on a highly competitive domestic market, before dominating world markets. Japan's global position in these sectors was strengthened by a degree of coopera-tion and synergy between large Japanese companies in associated sectors. In particular between electrical engineering firms, electronics and consumer electronics companies (Matsushita, Sony, Sharp and Sanyo), computing and telecoms companies (Fujitsu, NEC, Oki Electric), and several giant firms spanning two or more of these sectors (Toshiba, Hitachi, Mitsubishi Electric)(Cortazzi, 1994; Fruin, 1992).

Another renown force in Japan are the '*sogo shosha*' or international trading companies, like Itochu, Marubeni, Sumitomo, Mitsui and Mitsubishi (there are 9 in all), which played a major role in bringing Japanese products to the world markets. Also, the large Japanese banks, which in asset terms dominate the world rankings, including Dai-ichi Kangyo Bank, Sumitomo Bank, Fuji Bank and Sakura Bank. Commercial banks in Japan have always been oriented more towards corporate clients than individual customers compared to Western banks. Each has a significant influence over a specific range of companies and a clear role within a *keiretsu* group (a group of associated firms which share a close business relationship). Unlike arms-length shareholders in the West, with short-term repayment horizons, Japanese banks and other shareholders (usually affiliated companies, suppliers, distributors or associated companies) will have built a long-term commitment to supporting individual companies and their employees.

These and other distinctive features characterise the growth of the Japanese economy and still form part of its current structure, despite significant recent changes which will be discussed later in this chapter. A short summary of some key elements provides some background for the company case-studies discussed later.

Economic history

As in the case of West Germany the need to entirely rebuild Japan's industrial economy during the post-war period provided an opportunity for radical restructuring, especially in manufacturing, and renewed growth based on low expectations, cheap labour and foreign investment and expertise. Economic planners also established clear-cut development initiatives for a 'pursuer' mode of growth, including copying and adapting technology, products and processes from leading Western economies. This also laid the emphasis on market share rather than profits for Japanese companies and on constant upgrading of quality and quality control methods to match Western levels. Other factors included the lack of domestic resources which prompted a focus on value-added manufacturing and the low level of defence spending, allowing the Government to promote industrial development solely for commercial purposes.

'Cooperative competition' in domestic markets

Domestic markets in Japan are highly competitive, especially in sectors where the Japanese are strong internationally, such as autos, electronics, steel and machine tools. The country has, for example, 9 indigenous car manufacturers while the USA has only three (and the UK now has none). It also has 10 large electronics groups and over 115 companies producing machine tools, again far more per capita than the USA. Tough markets at home pushed Japanese companies to cut costs and emphasise quality, personal service and buyer-led product customization, all of which came to underlie their global competitiveness during later periods of export-driven growth. Toyota, for example, initially pioneered lean production techniques in the 1950s as a way of lowering costs to undercut local competitors, not to promote international competitiveness.

Paradoxically, Japanese firms are also highly 'cooperative', interactive and interdependent within Japan (although less so in recent times). It is generally recognised by firms in associated businesses that their corporate fortunes are tied together in an inter-linked system. This mutual obligation is underscored by the system of cross-shareholdings that bind firms within defined groups. It is estimated that anywhere between 65 percent and 80 percent of any Japanese company's shares are held by other Japanese companies with which it does business (specific forms of *keiretsu* groupings are described shortly).

Strong semi-official business organisations have grown up in Japan to support cooperation and coordination at several levels of business networks. These range from the national level, including Keidanren (the association of big businesses), Keizai Doyukai (the 'club' of senior executives), Nikkeiren (national federation of employers) and Nissho (the chambers of commerce representing smaller businesses), down to specialised industry sector associations and related consortia, with considerable influence over standards enforcement and aspects of entry and 'membership' in certain sectors of economic activity.

Allegiance to a common culture and a strong education system

Although cultural factors are often over-emphasised in discussions of Japanese economic strength, there are some distinctive social elements that underlie the country's success. A strong sense of 'groupism' or collectivism rather than individualism tends to dominate most aspects of Japanese life. Whether work-related or outside work, clubs, societies and specialist organisations exist at all levels and people will tend to belong to several, with a distinct ranking in each according to its focus and their age and experience.

Associated with this Japan has a strong education system characterised by a centrally-regulated curriculum (dominated by Monbusho, the Ministry of Education, Science and Culture), conformist attitudes amongst pupils, teachers and parents, high standards, and a focus on factual learning and the sciences. There is a significant amount of competition to get into good schools but a lack of competition between pupils once in school ('the nail that sticks out will be hammered down' is a local saying frequently used to describe this conformity). There is also a strong correlation between the level and *place* of education and job opportunities for school or university leavers, particularly at the top-end of the business and civil service hierarchies. About 38 percent of Japanese attend university and only one-third of the 480 Japanese universities are public (Cortazzi, 1994).

Government role

As more and more detailed studies are carried out to examine the relationship between government and industry in Japan, and its current role is re-evaluated within Japan, a clearer picture of the government's influence over the economic development process during the 1960s and 1970s is emerging. In the growth years the Japanese government, primarily through the mighty MITI (the Ministry of International Trade and Industry) and the Ministry of Finance (MOF), was able to influence market forces without completely overriding them. It managed, for example, to provide an overall direction for R&D and innovation at the national level but left companies and the process of competition to 'pick the winners'. They helped in the process of acquiring and adapting specific areas of technology and expertise from abroad while protecting local firms during the 'incubation' period in the 1950s. A significant amount of MITI's power, before the 1960s, stemmed from its control over foreign exchange allocations and influence over how credit was extended to different companies and sectors. It has arguably been on the wane since then.

We now know that government influence varied immensely by sector and project and much of the time it brokered firm-firm cooperation and applied subtle legislative controls to influence industrial development rather than engaging in direct intervention or funding (although it did some of this as well). MITI, for example played a strong role in the development of telecoms and industrial electronics capabilities through its relationship with NTT and the major electronics firms, but had little part to play in the development of consumer electronics where firms like Sony and Matsushita were entirely market-led (Fransman, 1995).

While the activities of MITI and MOF are well known in international policy making circles those of Monbusho, broadly defined as the Ministry of Education, Science and Culture and MPT, the Ministry of Posts and Telecommunications, are less renown. The former has had a strong grip on regulating Japan's strictly synchronised and widely praised school system. According to most Japanese teachers it rules with an iron hand, giving very little leeway for individual changes in the format, style or substance of the national curriculum. MPT's influence has always extended further into the Japanese economy and society than most foreigners realise. It has been in the limelight in recent years because of the growing calls for telecoms deregulation, breaking down the national NTT monopoly, and because of changes arising from the evolution of multimedia technologies and markets directly affecting its areas of responsibility. But MPT, as well as delivering the nation's mail, also runs Japan's largest savings system, with postal savings accounts worth over £74 billion (in March 1994), and the largest insurance company in the world, putting it in direct (though biased) competition with banks, private financial services and insurance companies.

The government-industry relationship encompasses the whole range of private and public sector institutions, from banks and financial organisations to universities and schools. Amongst various mechanisms that help coordinate decision-making and maintain the 'consensus' across these institutions is the practice of *amakudari* ('descent from heaven') involving the continual movement of senior politicians and civil servants from the public sector into companies and private sector organisations, often as highly paid 'consultants'.

The final distinctive characteristic of the Japanese economy, Japanese companies and corporate networks, deserves its own section.

Japanese companies

Partly as a result of the above underlying factors, from its economic history to specific forms of government intervention, Japan's industrial infrastructure and its corporations have developed along lines that are distinct from their Western counterparts. Some of the better-known characteristics of this very specific form of enterprise are described below.

Keiretsu

The renown Japanese corporate groupings, or *keiretsu*, characterised by cross-shareholdings and regular meetings between executives, represent more-or-less closely tied groups of integrated businesses. All evolved from the pre-war *zaibatsu* groups and some (Mitsui, Mitsubishi and Sumitomo) are direct descendants of these centrally-organised conglomerates and are now known as 'horizontal' *keiretsu*. The top six of these alone account for about 5 percent of the Japanese labour force and 16 percent of total Japanese corporate sales. Other *zaibatsu*-type *keiretsu* are centred on the Fuji, Sanwa and Daiichi Kangyo banks. These are often seen as distinct from the newer keiretsu which are headed by large manufacturers (Hitachi, Matsushita Electric Industrial, Toyota and NEC, for example) and tend to belong to a particular sector. A third type of grouping is recognised by some experts as distribution-centred, comprised of established networks of retailers and wholesalers that deal in a specific set of goods and services.

Unlike the European form of conglomerate Japanese groupings do not have a centralised holding company responsible for strategy across the group and as such they evolve in a more 'organic' way and are less vulnerable to hostile take-over. Companies may be multiple members across the three types of groupings outlined above but there are distinct power relationships between companies and groups and the largest firms dominate in a strongly hierarchical manner. Intra-group business relationships tend to be strongest in the manufacturing-centred *keiretsu* with up to 40 percent of some companies business carried out with other group members. This forms the basis of the strong, long-term relationships between manufacturers and preferred sub-contractors in Japan.

Mitsubishi is said to be the most tightly woven *keiretsu,* based in Tokyo's business district, Marunouchi, which as a result is also called 'Mitsubishi Village'. It has over 216,000 employees in businesses ranging through the financial, manufacturing, services and trading sectors from heavy engineering and oil to aerospace and beer. The 29 companies at the heart of the group hold an average of 38 percent of each others shares, a high proportion even for Japanese corporate groups. These companies exchange directors, cross-finance one-another and engage in joint-investment and cooperative research projects for the benefit of the whole group. Information exchange and inter-firm coordination is initiated at the most senior level when the bosses of the 29 core firms meet at the 'Friday Club' for lunch in Marunouchi each month (Dawkins, 1994a).

Behind each group of large companies in Japan there lies a huge network of smaller, affiliated sub-contractors and suppliers that are often ignored in analyses of Japan's domestic economy. The close long-term relationships between these suppliers and the larger manufacturers contributes both to the efficiency of Japanese industry and the closed nature of its economy. Taking Matsushita as an example it has around 500 prime contractors, or first-level suppliers, and over 6,000 smaller suppliers at lower levels of what is known as a 'co-prosperity' pyramid or cooperative manufacturing *keiretsu*. Even SMEs at the lower levels may rely on two or three top customers for over 50 percent of their revenue, making them both highly 'cooperative' (ie. 'willing' to change component price or specifications to the buyers requirements at short notice) and highly dependent on the fortunes of manufacturers higher up the hierarchy.

Alongside these corporate groupings are the influential trade associations and other business organisations, with the 'Keidanren' ('federation of economic organisations') at the top of the tree, dominated by the largest and most prestigious companies and with a considerable influence over national economic policy (the CBI is the closest parallel in the UK but does not match the power of the Keidanren). The 'Nikkeiren' ('federation of employers') and 'Nissho' (Japan Chamber of Commerce and Industry) are also fairly influential. Trade associations exist for practically every product, service and industry sector in Japan and wield a considerable but focused influence (and often have a restricted membership or are expensive to join). They generally cut-across *keiretsu* groupings and bring together corporate competitors, suppliers groups, distributors and Government agencies all under one affiliation based around a sector or product group. Prominent examples are the Electronics Industries Association of Japan (EIAJ) and the Japan Pharmaceutical Wholesalers Association (JPWA), which a foreign company, selling products in these markets would have to get to know.

There are around 1,500 trade associations in Japan covering an estimated 90 percent of the nation's market. They perform a key role in gathering information and data on specific markets, companies and products, including details on relevant regulation and legislation. They also monitor and strongly influence any changes in government policies pertaining to their particular sector, including trade and import regulations. Because they provide a forum for interaction between companies, and between companies and relevant government agencies, they act as a semi-official mechanism by which local companies can monitor, promote and restrict the activities of foreign companies in Japan.

Distribution, retailing and customer-orientation

As important as industry groups are the multi-layered distribution and retail networks which SMEs in particular find difficult to bypass. It is estimated that there is one retail outlet for every 75 people in Japan (over twice the USA ratio) and over 476,000 wholesale stores (Asahi Shimbun, 1995). These are organised both by region and by sector and product across Japan and tend to be geared to the large number of small retailers that serve the local markets (until recently, protected by government regulations). This 'tied' system of distribution, bound by strong face-to-face ties between sellers and buyers at each level, adds substantial costs to the final product. The American Chamber of Commerce in Japan (ACCJ) found out that over 48 percent of home electronics products in Japan are sold through exclusively affiliated stores, and about 99 percent of cars are distributed through exclusive dealerships (Terazono, 1994a; Economist, 1994).

To sell nation-wide for example it is common for a producer to have to deal with 8 or more different regional distributors each with three or more levels of wholesaler below them dividing the market by product or sub-region before reaching the retailer and finally the consumer. In many of Japan's consumer markets the large number of middlemen is the main reason behind the excessively high prices charged to the final consumer. Moreover, the distance that this creates between the producer and the final consumer creates a considerable dependence on established trading and distribution companies, giving them sustainable leverage in the market.

Through their control over the limited amount of valuable shelf space in Japan retailers are powerful determinants of which products get the chance to sell and which do not. They can be very difficult to deal with directly, particularly as it is common practice for retailers to return goods that they think will not appeal to customers, or that are not selling well, without payment. Smaller retailers also belong to strong 'street associations' called *shotengai* through which they market their stores and lobby at the local and regional levels. There has been a growing battle for some time between the small, more traditional neighbourhood shops ('mom-and-pop stores') and the large retailers, and discount stores like Daiei, with much of the controversy focusing on the 'Large Scale Retail Law' or 'Large Store Law' (Japan Times, 1994).

The high cost of Japan's distribution system has been described in terms of the so-called '1-5 ratio'. Where in the UK a product would be sold at £5 to the main distributor and end up costing around £10 to the final customer (obviously varied according product and sector), in Japan it would cost around £25 to the final customer - ie. final costs to the customer tend to be around 4-5 times ex-factory costs, again, obviously varying a great deal by sector and product.

In effect it is the customers who pay for the relatively closed, imperfect market that has developed in Japan, paying around 80 percent more than Westerners for most goods (Sazanami et al., 1995; Economist, 1995). To a great extent it is said to be manufacturers that have been responsible for maintaining high retail prices via the 'informally agreed pricing structure' which has, up until recently, produced a steady stream of profits for all . Now, increasingly, manufacturers are following an 'open market pricing' system, leaving retailers to set prices. Some of these changes are described in the next part of Chapter 2.

In terms of company-to-company sales and sub-contracting relationships there may also be a range of middle-men through which a producer must deal. More often the 'tied' or long-term sub-contractor relationships that are also a well-known feature of Japan's domestic economy favour existing suppliers and particularly corporate 'family' members. Foreign SMEs that are new to the market and are not known to large Japanese firms are least likely to be taken on as sub-contractors.

Until recently the strong 'patriotic' preferences of the average Japanese consumer and, perhaps, the average Japanese middle-manager responsible for company purchasing policy, provided a firm basis for the country's industrial and distribution infrastructure. Outside the luxury or branded consumer goods markets (Laura Ashley clothes, whisky from Scotland, Harrod's foods and so on) the Japanese have a strong preference for Japanese products. They believe them to be of the highest quality, as do consumers in other countries according to a Gallup poll of 20,000 people in 20 countries, which rated Japanese goods number one in this regard (and British goods fourth after the US and Germany). The same poll also put Japanese consumer patriotism at the top of the list, with 76 percent of Japanese respondents rating Japanese goods as very good or excellent, ahead of foreign goods from Germany (49 percent) and Britain (39 percent) (Bozell-Gallup, 1994; Tomkins, 1995). As discussed earlier, however, the buying preferences of the Japanese public are currently changing quite significantly, with the growing realisation that they have been paying over the odds for many goods and services because of the structure of the domestic market.

R&D

The most recent data available shows that Japan spends over 3.5 percent of national income on R&D, a little higher than the US figure and far higher than the UK figure (Morimoto, 1995). The most striking difference is the proportion of R&D expenditure made by the government compared to industry in these countries. In Japan about 18 percent of R&D is funded from government sources and 76 percent from private industries (plus 5 percent from universities), compared to government contributions of around 45 percent in the USA and 37 percent in the UK. Hitachi, Toyota, Matsushita, NEC and Fujitsu, the top 5 R&D spenders in Japan, spend as much (in terms of purchasing power parity) as the total R&D expenditure of the entire private sector in Britain (Fransman, 1992).

Japanese companies also lay the emphasis on the 'downstream' 'D' in R&D, including technology transfer, adaptation and commercialisation rather than more 'upstream' basic ('blue sky') research activities. Incremental innovation rather than radical or research-based 'invention' and market-driven product development rather than research-driven development characterise Japanese R&D investment. This also incorporates a large amount of 'blue-collar' R&D which is incremental innovation on the factory floor that is not recorded in official R&D statistics but has a significant impact on competitiveness. This is supported by the high status of engineers and scientists in Japanese companies (these will be the key decision-makers far more often than accountants or financial experts that tend to dominate large UK firms). There is also an emphasis in Japan on information collection and dissemination as value-added activities in their own right rather than as residual activities, particularly as regards technical information. Company-company and company-government collaboration and joint research initiatives are also more common at the pre-commercial stage than in the West.

The above statistics, however, under-emphasise the important coordinating role played by the Japanese Government agencies at the heart of a highly successful 'national innovation system'. MITI has played an important liaison role between government and companies, but in terms of expenditure on science and technology it is a minor player next to Monbusho (the ministry responsible for Education, Science and Culture) and the Science and Technology Agency (STA), which respectively account for 46 percent and 26 percent of funding next to MITI's 12 percent. Others, such as the Ministry of Post and Telecommunications and the Ministry of Construction, have also been very influential in their specific sectors.

Japan has arguably gone through the transition from being a net importer of technology to being a net exporter and there is now a growing emphasis on more 'upstream', basic research activities, both in companies and in a government keen to enhance Japan's international standing in this regard. To an extent this has brought into question the style of basic education and some aspects of company training in Japan which tend not to develop creativity and initiative but conformity and a lack of inventiveness.

Manufacturing

A vast number of books and studies are available that describe and attempt to explain the Japanese prowess in manufacturing. The following provides the most basic review of some of the key distinguishing characteristics of Japanese manufacturing firms. The most detailed comparative studies involving Japanese manufacturers have been carried out in the auto sector looking, for example, at productivity, manufacturing efficiency, design quality, return on R&D, product strategy and so on (such as Womack, Jones and Roos, 1990). The success of Japanese firms in this sector is shown by the fact that on average (up until the end of the 1980s) they produced new models of cars with only 55 percent of the engineering hours required by US and European manufacturers, maintaining development lead times that were over 15 months shorter, and sold them at a retail price that was, on average, 30 percent lower than competing models from the US and Europe (Cusumano and Nobeoka, 1992).

A variety of attributes underlie Japanese manufacturing competitiveness and while detailed accounts can be found in numerous other sources some of the main ones are listed here:

-   attention to quality (built in at every stage of development and production processes), often formalised in quality circles (QC) but related much more to the individual employees concern for flawless output

-   strong manufacturer-component supplier linkages (coordinated initial development and subsequent innovation), again formalised within just-in-time type systems but reliant for their success on the close, informal relationships between buyers and suppliers

-   ability to cut production costs (using advanced manufacturing technology, 'just-in-time', and flexible and 'lean' manufacturing techniques etc.)

-   higher degree of credibility and responsibility given to engineers and technical expertise

Organisation and culture

We can continue the above list with some of the main characteristics of the 'generic Japanese' management style, upon which the above manufacturing competencies are based:

-   effective communications internally and with outside firms (decentralized, horizontal information flows)

-   less separation of R&D, design, manufacturing and marketing functions

-   life-time employment tradition, (use of 'voice' rather than 'exit'), low wage differentials between workers and managers, plus, job-rotation within the firm and strong emphasis on training on-the-job

-   managers as problem-definers, not firefighters and as educators and mentors, not disciplinarians

-   strong group/team ethic, loyalty and motivation combined with competitiveness between teams

-   strict 'formal' hierarchy (based on seniority) combined with strong underlying 'informal' networks and a tendency towards consensus-based ('*nemawashi*' and '*ringi*') decision-making (high-fliers within the firm tend to get 'horizontal promotion' such as a temporary foreign posting, plus there is a lack of 'lateral entry' ie. outsiders entering firm at senior level)

-      general 'long-termism,' focus on growth and employment stability (and market share) rather than profits and shareholder dividends

These are obviously generalisations, or factors which tend to exist more-or-less in a wide range of Japanese firms. Overall, Japanese firms have a strong focus on human resources. A great deal of their strength (and perhaps a source of some weaknesses) lies in the employer-employee relationship and the commitment and loyalty shown by each to the other.

Similarly, at the broader level employees, companies and networks of companies in Japan should not be viewed as 'commodities' in the way that financially-minded Western managers might view them. Their value (and their ability to 'add value' to products and services so efficiently) is built on the unwritten loyalties between managers, employees, shareholders and between companies themselves. These relationships and ties are not a spin-off from economic activity but are central to it and have a commercial value that stock markets cannot 'account' for and (most) economists fail to incorporate in models of rational decision-making behaviour and perfect markets. Failure to understand this and adapt to it on first entering the Japanese market was a major stumbling block for many of the firms examined for this study.

This brief overview of some of the key characteristics of the Japanese economy has been highly selective and deliberately focused on the Japanese enterprise. Issues like the nature of corporate groupings (*keiretsu*), the complex distribution hierarchies, large firms' strong R&D and the 'classic' manufacturing strengths identified in specific Japanese companies have been covered because they have a direct relevance for foreign firms doing business in Japan. There are many other books and articles that give a detailed account of various aspects of the Japanese economy, society, culture and political system.

The distinctiveness of Japanese companies and corporate networks in Japan has been summed up as the '3 M's' in an excellent book called 'Kaisha' ('company') by Abegglen and Stalk. These are:

-      marketing: direct links with consumers via retailers and wholesalers and strong customer-led product development;
-      money: cross-shareholding and the lack of outside pressure for short-term returns and stock price improvements, and;
-      manpower strategy: worker involvement, loyalty, effective teamworking and devolvement of responsibility combined with hierarchy (Abegglen and Stalk, 1985).

The features listed in this chapter so far indicate some of the more obvious differences between Japan and the West. There are clearly many variations on these basic themes and no strict rules. Stereotypical views of Japan's economic infrastructure, companies and managers still abound, despite the growing volume of more detailed and insightful studies in recent years. A critical initial mistake made by many newcomers to Japan is to base their dealings with the Japanese on what they have heard in the West rather than on what they observe in Japan.

Similarly facts, figures and commentaries on the growth and current strengths of Japan, and the perceived threat it poses to the West, are all too often based on stereotypical views. Few have examined key areas of weakness in the economy, such as its poor aerospace industry, relatively uncompetitive chemicals and pharmaceuticals sectors and various specific inefficiencies within Japanese companies. For example, according to a study carried out by McKinsey management consultants examining manufacturing productivity by worker, Japan has a clear lead in internationally-traded goods such as cars, steel and consumer electronics but outside these sectors other economic systems produce a superior performance. In brewing for example US workers produce half again as many pints per head as the Japanese and in food manufacturing Japan's output per hour worked is only a third of America's. This is, in part, due to local protectionism and the weakness of retailers in Japan which create inefficiencies in the local market. In brewing and food manufacturing the Japanese export little and resist the influx of imports leaving these sectors protected from the pressures of global competition.

The many inefficiencies of white-collar management and office staff organisation are being increasingly recognised as much of the success of Japanese firms is traced to blue-collar operations. In particular, wasted office time and over-bureaucratic procedures, low use of IT (in 1993 only one office worker in 10 had a PC on his or her desk and only 9 percent of these were networked, compared to 52 percent in the USA), loss of creativity and entrepreneurship (through conformism and loyalty) and misuse of women-power are serious deficiencies.

More of Japan's weaknesses have come to light in the recent recession. In addition to (and sometimes because of) the economic changes taking place Japan is now going through a period of significant social and political upheaval. These 'creative gales of destruction' have far-reaching consequences for Japanese companies and the Japanese people which they are only starting to come to grips with and as such they have significant implications for foreign companies wanting to do business with Japan and within Japan.

A changing nation

The past few years have seen a number of major changes in Japan's social, economic and political structure, and there are more on the way. Instability is not welcomed by any nation, but the added difficulties brought about in Japan by the current period of 'chaotic upheaval' is partly related to the unusual degree of stability and consensus that the country has experienced throughout a long 'high-growth' era that most observers believe is now over.

Economic recession and recovery

In the early 1990s Japan experienced its worst economic recession since the oil shock of the early 1970s and in some respects its worst in the post-war period. Slower growth, reduced investment, declining property prices, increased unemployment are all secondary effects of earlier declines in profitability, increased domestic costs and falling domestic demand. These were masked in the late 1980s by rapid growth rates based on strong exports and cheap capital which ended abruptly when the 'bubble burst' and *endaka* began. The recessionary cycle is linked to the fast appreciation of the Yen, which partly resulted from the 1985 Plaza Accord but continued until mid-1995, rising 24 percent in value between early 1993 and early 1995.

Despite rationalisation and consolidation in key sectors Japanese companies are still having to substantially restructure their operations in the face of longer term pressures, including: more expensive capital; growing competition from low-cost Asian producers; declining prices of key manufactures, particularly electronics and autos; a slowing domestic economy and growing inroads into the domestic economy by foreign competitors.

Because a large proportion of Japanese SMEs are sub-contractors to larger companies (56 percent according to one source), within a complex, multi-tiered hierarchy, recession and reorganisation amongst the giants (discussed in the following section) has had a direct effect on a large number of SMEs. Restructuring effects, coupled with the appreciation of the Yen have created knock-on effects all the way through this hierarchy, from primary (direct) sub-contractors through second, third and fourth-level indirect suppliers. Mazda, for example, is attempting to cut its first-line sub-contractors from 62 companies to 16, thereby passing on the responsibility for pushing down input prices to companies further down the chain and leaving a host of dependent SMEs to find other markets (Dawkins, 1994a).

Corporate reorganisation

Many of the changes being forced on Japanese managers are, like the eventual opening up of Japan's rice market, culturally taboo but economically inevitable. One of the most significant is the erosion of the life-time employment system which is likely to continue even after Japan's full economic recovery takes place and unemployment, which reached higher levels (some say double) at its peak than was indicated by the 'official' rate of three percent, begins to fall.

The initial reaction to the recession was to treat falling profits as part of a cyclical trend which companies could weather using their momentum from the previous decade. Japanese managers had little experience of how to handle the radical restructuring and 'downsizing' that became necessary, particularly the problem of labour costs that quickly began to erode domestic manufacturing competitiveness. Labour costs per head in manufacturing were 25 percent higher in 1992 than in 1988, in part because of the rise in white collar employment which expanded by a fifth between 1985 and 1992. Managers have been particularly slow in reorganising to overcome their own office and administrative inefficiencies and this, combined with their reticence in cutting employees, resulted in the rapid collapse of corporate earnings at the start of the down-turn (Schlender, 1994).

The erosion of the life-time employment system is shown by the growing number of redundancies, early-retirements, horizontal movement of employees, rising use of performance-related pay, and significantly reduced wage increases and bonuses at the annual wage negotiations. Examples include Honda and Fujitsu, both of which employed less than 20 percent of their usual intake of university graduates in 1993 and introduced merit-based remuneration schemes (Fisher, 1994). These changes are having a significant influence on Japanese society more broadly. They have already had considerable impact on the flexibility of the labour market in Japan and may well have long-term implications for aspects of the traditional employee-employer relationship, in-house training and company loyalty.

Companies have responded to the recession in other ways. Diversification strategies are the cornerstone of many corporate investment plans, a good example being the changes at NKK, Japan's second largest steelmaker. At the beginning of 1995 its previously loss-making marine engineering division turned in an operating profit of almost 15 percent on sales of £65.8 million (although NKK overall expects to make a loss of 5 times this amount). The turnaround in this particular division was due to extensive (and risky) investments into areas outside shipbuilding. These include the leisure industry, manufacturing an indoor ski slope and an artificial surfing beach ('Wild Blue'), using core technologies from their own test divisions. In addition to diversification within manufacturing the changing cost structure for industrial production has, in particular, accelerated the shift towards services.

Another much talked-about trend has been the reorganisation of subcontracting relationships and a general loosening of *keiretsu* group ties. There is evidence that the system of cross-shareholding is becoming increasingly diluted through reductions in mutual equity stakes. In their drive to cut costs large manufacturing firms in Japan are avoiding giving their usual suppliers a guaranteed volume of business over the long term but are encouraging them to compete with each other with a new emphasis on price as the deciding factor. Studies have shown that the average share of *keiretsu* members' sales to each other has fallen since 1989 and is continuing as imports become cheaper, particularly in competitive manufacturing sectors, such as autos. This has happened alongside a general move to reduce the number of parts used in standard products and reduce the variety of products and models manufactured, as well as cutting down on the rate of new product development.

The high-yen recession has also forced a change in the traditional convoluted supplier-distributor-retailer chain as prices have been pushed downward. On the one hand manufacturers are themselves having to source materials and inputs from abroad, as well as move new manufacturing facilities to cheaper overseas production locations. So a more price-driven domestic market and freer flows of cheaper imports is in their interest. On the other hand consumers are becoming increasingly price conscious and are therefore demanding more imported products. This demand is partly being met by discount stores which import directly and cover the whole distribution chain from manufacturer to final customer. A process of vertical integration is therefore taking place, more prominently in some sectors than others, consolidating the supply chain and reducing the final price of products.

This is happening alongside a decline in the use of exclusive agreements with single distributors or sales organisations. In the past these were the norm and in most sectors it was impossible to have multiple agreements or play distributors and retailers against each other to push up sales. Increasingly now multiple agreements are accepted and the trader-wholesaler-retailer link need not be tied but competitive, with many players competing at each level in a 'less imperfect' market.

Also as part of general corporate restructuring in Japan, higher domestic production costs are pushing firms to invest in facilities abroad, with a shift in foreign direct investment from Europe and the USA to Asian locations. This is especially difficult when local overcapacity and surplus stocks threaten Japanese jobs. Industrialists in Japan are already talking about the 'hollowing out' of their corporations in much the same way as American managers viewed the multinationalisation of their manufacturing firms in the early 1980s. Already about one-third of all cars and machines made by Japanese-owned companies are made outside Japan and almost a quarter of its manufacturing output is made abroad (a figure set to double over the next five years by some estimates). Japan has been overtaken by the USA as the largest producer of vehicles and by China as the largest producer of colour televisions (Japan is now a net importer). South Korea even took over the top spot (temporarily) from Japan in shipbuilding in 1993. The Export-Import Bank expects the percentage of production abroad to rise from 16.1 percent in 1993 to 21.6 percent in 1997 and a survey by the Japan Development Bank shows that manufacturing companies plan to increase investment overseas by 18 percent in the near future while decreasing investment in Japan by 9 percent. Although these trends will help the imbalance of trade through increased imports from the Asian countries that Japanese manufacturers are moving to they will adversely affect manufacturing employment in Japan (causing an increase from the current 3 percent level to 7 percent by 2000, according to the Sanwa Research Institute) (JETRO, 1995; Dawkins, 1995a; Nakamoto, 1995).

A telling example of all this was Nissan's closure of its 30-year-old Zama car plant near Tokyo in March 1995, the first Japanese car plant to be closed since the Second World War. Ironically, part of the plant that has made 11.2 million vehicles in its lifetime is to be turned into a pre-delivery inspection centre for Ford vehicles. Zama, with a local population of 116,000 has lost 2,500 jobs, although most have been moved elsewhere within Nissan or found jobs in local service industries.

Despite the depth and the significance of the recent recession for Japanese companies that did not have experience of such a down-turn there are now growing signs that companies are finally adapting to the new economic constraints and business activity is picking up. After all, Japanese firms have been coping with a rising currency for over 20 years (in 1972 the exchange rate was Y360 to the US Dollar) and with cost-cutting and reorganisation for over three years now and appear to be in better shape to benefit from the upturn. Renewed growth is particularly being driven by exports to the revived Western economies and even more to the rapidly growing Asian markets. Asia overtook the US as Japan's biggest export market in 1991 and now its exports to Asia exceed sales to the USA by well over a third in Dollar terms. Company profits, especially for electronics and precision instruments, began to turn around in 1994 and continue to improve (Dawkins, 1994b). Most analysts predict that Japanese firms will further adapt and continue to succeed and the Japanese economy will continue to be a crucial market to be involved in for foreign businesses.

Banking and financing changes

The changing role of banks and the evolution of Japan's financial services industry have recently created instability in the corporate finance system. Before the 1980s Japanese banks were responsible for over 85 percent of funds supplied to industry. During the 1980s there was a general move towards using capital markets for funding investment, particularly amongst large manufacturing companies in Japan. These used bonds and equity for about 52 percent of the finance they raised in 1989 compared to 27 percent in 1980. Partly as a consequence banking relationships became less stable with far more companies taking loans from more than one bank and changing their main lender. Loose financial discipline in the high growth, high investment years resulted in heavy depreciation charges, often on investments which have resulted in overcapacity rather than bringing in extra revenue.

The scale of this instability only became clear after the 'bubble-era' of the late 1980s when the collapse in property prices, which underpinned much of the private sector borrowing, left many companies in financial difficulties. Their problems have been highlighted by the growing number of non-performing loans and the loan restructuring carried out by the commercial banks (like Mitsubishi in June 1994 and Daiwa in mid-1995), who have also suffered as a result. The crisis continues, with land values in Japan's main cities having fallen by 50 percent between 1990 (the peak year) and 1995.

As a result, a process of consolidation, rationalisation and mergers is underway, partly forced on banks from Government organisations, as financial deregulation begins. The latest example from the land of the banking giants is the merger between Mitsubishi Bank and the Bank of Tokyo (March, 1995) to create the world's largest bank with assets of £514 billion. Smaller financial organisations have also come under considerable strain in recent years and are being encouraged to merge with larger partners to avoid collapsing under bad debt.

This process is exacerbating existing imbalances in the banking sector. 45 percent of the private sector domestic loan market is already held by the top 21 banks, the city, the long-term investment groups and the trust banks. The remaining 5,700 financial institutions share the other 55 percent. Japan's top 11 banks control a third of total lending to the Japanese economy and these have also been shaken by the burden of bad debts, with pre-tax profits falling for the fifth year running by an average of 41.6 percent (to March, 1994) (Financial Times, 1994; Terazono, 1994b).

A political system in transition

In the past the successful government-industry relationship in Japan has been founded on political stability and a clear delineation of the roles and responsibilities of the government and its ministerial bureaucracies, an arrangement built on the unquestioned dominance of the ruling Liberal Democratic party. For a number of reasons, including the well-publicised scandals involving unethical financial dealings amongst senior politicians and public calls for a more democratic system of government, this system became untenable in the early 1990s. Aspects of the traditional role of government in regulating, coordinating, and planning industrial activity and in fulfilling a wide range of socio-economic functions are increasingly being questioned.

In place of the long-standing single-party dominance a highly unstable coalition has emerged which has so far revealed the relatively unsophisticated nature (in international terms) of Japanese politics and which has significant implications for government-industry relations in the future. Alongside this 'top-down' realignment the government bureaucracies, who were largely responsible for the coherence of economic policies and the strength of policy-implementation in the 1960s and 1970s (particularly MITI, the Ministry of International Trade and Industry, and MOF, the Ministry of Finance), are being forced to accept a smaller say in managing the economy. These powerful bureaucracies have experienced a steadily declining level of control over the private sector for some time, with the most radical shifts of power in recent years. Although the bureaucrats (all 1.2 million of them) have tried to retain their past levels of interventionist powers, they are being pushed on the one hand by the politicians and on the other the businesses (via the Keidanren in particular) to deregulate the economy (Nakamoto, 1994a).

Pressure to deregulate from within has been less evident (though no less influential) than the pressure from the international economic community, in particular the USA, to reduce government control over the Japanese economy. But because government regulation and is seen to underlie to some degree the imbalance of trade and foreign direct investment (discussed in a following section) between Japan and its economic partners, the deregulation issue has taken on far greater political implications for Japan's 'identity' and position on the world stage than other 'internationalisation' issues.

Very crude estimates suggest that over 10,000 government regulations currently affect around 40 percent of industrial activity in Japan. To a greater or lesser extent these restrict flexibility and maintain inertia in an economic system now under pressure to undergo significant structural changes. Also to a greater or lesser extent these regulations tend to operate to the particular detriment of foreign firms operating in the domestic economy, although they are only one set of factors amongst many that affect foreign firms in Japan and cannot be singled out as being solely responsible for the country's imbalance of trade and FDI (Financial Times, 1995a).

Nonetheless, government-led deregulation is seen as a lever which foreign governments can lean on to put pressure on Japan to 'open its markets', again, despite the declining influence now enjoyed by the Japanese government over the private sector. Specific demands from US and European Community lobbyists, across a variety of sectors, include:

- an end to restrictions placed on the development of new supermarkets, which are holding back the growth of discount stores that act as outlets for cheaper imported products

- a loosening of foreign investment regulations that are helping maintain the low level of foreign involvement in Japan's financial markets (such as the tiny 0.2 percent share that foreign investment managers have of Japan's £1,075 billion pension fund market)

- a streamlining of the car inspection system which requires new vehicles to be checked twice by two different government agencies

- changes to the regulations supporting NTT's monopoly in the telecoms sector and an opening up of long-distance and local networks

- completion of the steps taken so far to open the government's own procurement practices, to open large contracts to overseas competition

The real level of government influence over the private sector in Japan and the effects of public-sector regulations on foreign companies in Japan was revealed more accurately in interviews with British SME managers for this study and will be discussed further in subsequent chapters of this book.

Taking a broad look at the Japanese political and economic system in its current state of flux, compared to its more solid past, it is evident that its has been significantly weakened. The 'iron triangle' of politicians, bureaucrats and businesses in the past acting as a coherent power centre, with all parties knowing who had what role and range of responsibilities and who had to be influenced to achieve this or that end. It was a structure with inherent mechanisms for focusing all efforts towards economic development at the national level. It has been replaced, at least temporarily, by uncertainty but also by a more flexible and dynamic system of government.

Social change

Economic and political change is inevitably tied to social change and it is difficult
to fully understand the nature of the economic and political transition that Japan
is currently going through without an understanding of the cultural and social
upheaval it is in the midst of. Moreover it is hard to appreciate the significance of
current social changes without an understanding of Japan's rich cultural heritage.

Religion has always played an important role in Japanese society and
underpins a number of distinct aspects of its form of economic organisation. The
nation's cultural roots lie in an amalgam of Confucianism and Buddhism, both
considerably adapted over the centuries into a unique 'philosophy for life', more
readily applied to everyday living than many aspects of Christianity. Confucianism (said to have been introduced in about 500BC) underlies two central social
'mores' in Japan, loyalty (*chu*) and obligation (*giri*) and is linked to the themes of
strong family, social hierarchy, ritualistic behaviour and politeness. It also
underlies the lower status of women in Japanese society. Buddhism, through the
'five precepts', the 'four noble truths' and the 'eightfold path', also prescribes certain
social and behavioural standards focusing on spiritual discipline and selflessness.

Before both Confucianism and Buddhism were introduced into Japan the
indigenous religion was Shinto ('the way of the gods'). This became bound up,
particularly with Buddhism, very early on and remains popular today as evidenced
by ritual parades for certain gods and the visiting of shrines. Other historical
influences have added to these foundation religions through the centuries,
including the introduction of Christianity in the 16th Century (adding to the
amalgam) and a strongly feudal or class-based society which dominated in the
Tokugawa period (1616-1853) up until the Meiji era (1868-1912) which laid the
basis for modern Japan (Cortazzi, 1993).

'State Shinto' was created in the late 19th Century in an attempt to unify all
religions within a kind of 'spiritual nationalism' under the 'divine' emperor. This
added a militaristic edge to many of the existing social institutions, emphasising
a blind devotion to one's superiors, and arguably reached a cult-like status at its
peak at the end of the Second World War. This has left, amongst other things a
strong form of right-wing extremism amongst some social and political groups as
well as a certain vulnerability to fringe cults, which are common in Japan.

In 1993 the government's cultural affairs agency estimated there were
231,000 religious groups in Japan, of which 40,000 or so lay outside the
mainstream religions of Buddhism, Shinto and Christianity. Some, like the Soka
Gakkai, with its strong political wing, the Komeito (the second largest political
party in Japan), are far from being on the fringe and have a strong influence at the

heart of Japanese society, politics and business. Others, that are further removed from the centre, are making their views known in a more explicit manner that ever before (like the Aum Shinri Kyo cult's gas attack on the Tokyo subway), creating greater social friction than has been felt for some time.

There is no doubt that the religious and cultural past described above remains a strong influence in modern Japanese society giving rise to a certain 'guiding spiritualism' as evidenced by aspects of Japanese behaviour, including ritual, hierarchy, loyalty, obligation, social cohesion, and so on. Many of these aspects of social behaviour are steeped in the language and invisible to most '*gaijin*' or outsiders.

There is also no doubt that Western and other 'outside' influences have created fundamental changes in Japanese society and this is currently causing an unprecedented degree of tension between traditional and modern ways of living. There is no time to go into the broader elements of social change, which include the aging population, changing diet and changing health problems, a rising crime rate (though from a very low base rate), new attitudes to work and leisure and, amongst some in Japan, a perceived decline in moral values (amongst others, a new freedom and social openness). We will focus here, and later in this book, on the implications of such change for foreign businesses in Japan.

Some of the most obvious changes, and clear evidence of the trend towards Western tastes, are in the buying patterns of Japanese consumers. Part of this is the move to Western foods and clothing styles, which has been going on for some time. More recently there has also been a change in the types of products the Japanese are willing to buy and where they are willing to buy them from. Following the high-spending, brand-conscious eighties, there is a growing preference for 'value for money' and an increase in buying from hitherto frowned upon discount retail stores. This is partly because of current recessionary pressure on wages but also an indication that consumers are beginning to realise and object to the fact that Japan's consumer prices are still on average over 80 percent above the OECD average.

This change in consumer behaviour has challenged the multi-layered distribution system that has dominated wholesale and retail networks of family-run stores in Japan and has resulted in an expensive, inflexible supplier infrastructure tied to local manufacturers. A flatter distribution system has begun to develop, providing consumers with the opportunity to buy imports more directly, at cheaper prices. The Daiei chain, an example of one store group leading this change, experienced a boom in its own label brands early in 1994 allowing it to cut prices by using imported products, from Brazilian orange juice to Korean video tapes.

These and other recent changes in the Japanese economy will be discussed further in later parts of this book in terms of their implications for British companies operating in Japan.

A changing international role

As a parallel, in some respects, to the internal tension between 'traditionalists' and 'progressives' regarding the social and cultural norms governing Japan, there is a tension in terms of its foreign policy, between those who cling to its more nationalist and 'isolationist' past and those who look to Japan becoming better integrated in the global economy and fulfilling a more prominent role in the international arena in the future. In particular the latter involves moving to a less dependent or subordinate relationship with the USA in terms of trade and economics, which the average Japanese is very much in favour of. But it also means Japan sharing a proportion of the global responsibilities more commensurate with its economic power and being more accountable to international governance organisations (the United Nations, the World Trade Organisation and others), which many Japanese are wary of.

A range of key issues that have been debated over and again in Japan in recent years illustrate these tensions. In particular, the question of rice imports, with Japanese farmers, on a par with the strong agricultural lobby in the USA, representing traditional values of the past, while mainly trying to protect their own livelihoods through protectionism. Also on several occasions in recent years the question of whether to send Japanese troops to accompany UN peacekeepers in various parts of the globe repeatedly has acted as test case of changing attitudes and expectations of Japan's international role and the political resolve to distance themselves from the nitty-gritty of global responsibility.

Unfortunately for Japan in some ways is the fact that where it is playing a leading role it is not fully noticed. An important example is Japan's position as the world's largest aid donor to developing countries (it 'gave' over $10 billion in 1995), a position it has held for the last 6 years. Although over 65 percent of this aid has gone to Asia, and despite criticisms that much of it is 'tied aid' linking loans to contracts for Japanese companies, it is taking too long for Japan to take its rightful place at centre stage amongst countries and organisations that set the political and economic agenda for aid and relations with developing countries. Japan is only just beginning to have an influence within the World Bank and the International Monetary Fund and has only recently begun to challenge (albeit in a small way) the Western assumptions governing aid programmes, which mainly stem from US and European historical domination of international relations. This is partly connected to Japan's own lack of an institutional infrastructure, expertise and research in this field (now rapidly changing), but it is also related to Western recognition that development assistance is directly linked to political patronage and global power.

So far Japan has been reaping many of the benefits arising from the economic growth of S-E Asia but has remained reliant on the USA's military and 'policing' role, such as in the case of North Korean aggression. The question of whether Japan should 're-arm' in any sense has not really been discussed as a serious option by other dominant countries and does not appear to be favoured by the majority of Japanese.

Japan's past aggressions in Asia still haunt the national consciousness and hamper the coherence of the entire region as a political and economic alliance. This is not helped by its failure to fully face up to these aggressions, despite the growing pressure at the grass roots level (such as from so-called 'ex-comfort' women) and from senior political levels. It was brought to a head during the VJ Day celebrations in Europe in mid-1995 and Murayama's muted apology, which brought to light the growing nationalist movement within Japan, at all levels of society. This movement is tied up with a fear of cultural absorption or Westernisation in Japan and the loss of Japan's own uniqueness. It has prompted a strong revival in *'nihonjinron'* (a field of study that attempts to define the essence of Japaneseness) and support for a more independent, proud and assertive political establishment to reflect Japanese success and achievement, rather than humbling failure or past mistakes.

On the other hand, more broadly, there is a degree of forgive and forget, and the bridge-building process in Asia is being helped along by the coincidence of economic interests between Japan and its poorer (but cheaper) neighbours. Japanese companies, looking for low-cost manufacturing sites, are offering the jobs, technologies, training and investment that are the lifeblood of the current economic 'miracle' in the first-tier NICs (Newly Industrialising Countries, such as South Korea, Taiwan and Singapore) and their second-tier cousins (like Vietnam and China). It is this trade-off that will hopefully eclipse past confrontations and focus all interests on economic success.

The signs are that Japan is becoming more and more involved in behind-the-scenes economic and political coordination in the Asia-Pacific region (partly via APEC). Through a combination of aid, growing FDI and intra-regional trade, plus a growing sense of shared political futures, the region is evolving into a coherent power bloc, in which Japan is likely to play an increasingly explicit coordinating role.

The future?

Some of the major areas of social, political and economic change now affecting Japan have been reviewed above. Despite the fundamental nature of the changes Japan is experiencing, its people have a stronger sense of 'nationhood' than most, giving it a firm base from which to adapt. Although the transition period is bringing to light many of the country's weaknesses, many of which existed before but were obscured by its dazzling economic success, it will no doubt emerge from this period with new strengths.

It is likely to have a more open and mature political system, although how long this will take to emerge is difficult to foresee. A lengthy transition to an effective and efficient democratic system, with newly-balanced roles for politicians, civil servants and business leaders would be a severe disadvantage considering the critical decisions that now need to be made in terms of both domestic economic management and Japan's international role. Social change is linked to political change and the essential maturing process of the country's political infrastructure requires the active involvement of its people in the political process and institutions.

This relates to one of the many pressing social issues that face the Japanese people themselves and one which will be brought into the open more often as public debate becomes more accepted. The strong, evolving tensions amongst people of different ages and regions, their customs, institutions, and social and political affiliations are becoming more obvious. Japan's social homogeneity has proved to be a strength in the period of rapid economic development of the past, but may well prove increasingly to be a weakness as it becomes more international. As the country becomes less isolated from the rest of the world the individualistic, Western aspirations of the younger Japanese increasingly clash with the more conservative, group-oriented nature of the older Japanese. The latter are largely responsible for the rapid economic development of Japan in the post-war period through their hard work and their emphasis on building rather than enjoying prosperity.

The youth of Japan, and many of its increasingly well-travelled middle-aged citizens, are now pushing at the social restrictions that emphasise education, training and work above personal pleasure, leisure and family. At the same time a greater degree of interaction with other countries and cultures, plus a growing number of foreigners visiting, working and living in Japan, are forcing many Japanese to compromise what has been termed their 'ethnocentric' view of the world.

Such changes, follow in some respects (over an accelerated time-scale) those which have taken place in the Western economies in the recent and distant past. In economic terms they may also leave Japan with some of the weaknesses of the West, in the face of the growing threat from the Newly Industrialising Countries of S.E.Asia and China. Japan is no longer a cost-effective location for manufacturing activities and this is unlikely to change, no matter how much re-organisation is carried within Japanese companies. So while these companies may well adapt over the next few years to the rigours of a more open market system and greater degree of integration in terms of trade with the rest of the world economy, they will join with the West in finding many of their current comparative advantages eaten away by 'hungry' newcomers.

At the same time the service sector in Japan is on the rise and, since the middle of 1994, employs more people than manufacturing. This heralds a range of important structural changes that are about to take place, potentially propelling the Japanese economy into the kind of service boom that transformed the US economy in the 1980s (Dawkins, 1995b).

Selling to Japan; investing in Japan

Moving on from a general description of Japan, past, present and future, this section will focus more on Japan's trade relations with the rest of the world to provide a more specific background to our survey of UK SMEs in Japan. The experience of British SMEs, described later, shows that selling to Japan involves a considerable amount of up-front investment. Companies need to invest in an understanding of Japan, as well as investing time, money and effort in anticipation of rewards that are often difficult to quantify.

The statistics show that investment from Japan, by Japanese companies into other countries, significantly exceeds inward investment into Japan from other countries. Managers thinking about making this up-front investment are right to ask why this is so. Are there considerable barriers to trade and foreign investment in Japan? Is it worth trying to invest in Japan?

This next section reviews the statistics and describes how the situation in Japan is now changing, with more and more foreign firms looking to Japan's domestic markets and succeeding in exploiting the growing opportunities it offers.

The imbalance of trade and foreign direct investment

The much-talked about trade imbalance between Japan and the rest of the world is closely linked to the imbalance in flows of FDI. Both illustrate how relatively closed the Japanese economy has been until recently, compared to those of other major nations, and both also point to the current opportunities for foreign firms in Japan.

Trade In terms of its GNP Japan has traditionally had a low level of both imports (around 7 percent of GNP before the early 1990s) and, surprisingly, exports (around 9 percent of GNP) compared to most large economies. However, because of its enormous domestic economy, it was still the world's 3rd largest importer at the beginning of this decade, buying $235 billion-worth of goods, particularly food, raw materials and fuels. This was $52 billion less than it exported, as it tends to export value-added items such as motor vehicles, machinery and transport equipment, hence the massive imbalance. However, between 1985 and 1991 the value, in US dollar terms, of Japan's imports trebled, from $40.2 to $120.3 billion. In the same period manufactured goods, as a proportion of total imports, increased from 30 percent to 50 percent (in 1995 manufactured imports, valued at $94 billion, represented almost 58 percent of total imports).

Although Japan's merchandise trade surplus in 1994 hit a record high for the fourth year running (up 0.8 percent from the previous year to £77.6 billion) currency movements masked a real decline in the surplus. In real terms exports rose by 9.6 percent but imports rose by 14 percent. Then, between July 1994 and July 1995 exports grew 10.3 percent and imports by a surprising 28.6 percent, narrowing the trade imbalance significantly. The recent structural changes are brought home by the fact that in 1994, for the first time ever, imports overtook exports as a percentage of production in Japan at just under and just over 14 percent respectively (Dawkins, 1995b).

A closer look at Japan's trade figures show that the import-export imbalance has largely been due to relatively few specific sectors. Beyond these there is a much closer import-export ratio, indicating particular domestic markets in which foreign companies have been active for some time. Over 75 percent of Japanese exports in 1992 by value, according to MITI figures, came from exports of machinery and equipment, in particular automobiles, electronic and electrical products. Breaking this down even further it becomes clear that a significant part of Japan's export strength comes from the products that epitomise its industrial power, cars, VCRs, TVs, Hi-fi systems and electronic components. But it is a mistake to translate these specific strengths into comprehensive competitiveness across all sectors, as those who generalise about the Japanese economy on the basis of these specific sectors tend to do. (Interestingly, recent trade figures show that in 1994 the strongest export sectors for Japan were electronic parts, engines and motor parts. Car exports fell and car imports rose, up 38 percent by value, and imports of electronic parts and office computers also grew; Dawkins, 1995c.)

According to the Japanese Ministry of International Trade and Industry

(MITI) recent figures show that the UK lies 7th in the league of importers from Japan importing $12,286 million worth of goods and services. This is 3.6 percent of Japan's exports compared to 6 percent taken by Germany and over 28 percent bought by the USA. By contrast Britain is 14th in the top-20 list of exporters to Japan and is responsible for 2.1 percent of the country's imports, worth $4,889 million. Table (2.1) and Table (2.2) illustrate the most traded (visible) items between Japan and the UK from 1985 to 1993.

Despite the continued imbalance the UK is successfully exporting a growing volume of products to Japan, with total exports up by 13 percent in 1994, despite falling domestic demand and consumer spending in Japan. Moreover, the proportion of manufactured products exported is on the rise, including machinery and equipment (30 percent of total manufactured exports) and the future demand in Japan for such products is likely to grow. In 1994, despite this strong growth in exports to Japan, Britain still had the largest trade deficit with Japan of all the leading European economies. Preliminary figures for 1995 show a significant increase in UK exports to Japan (up 35 percent in the first half of the year by DTI calculations) (Owen, 1995), ahead of almost all of Japan's other Western trading partners.

UK-Japan trade: the top ten (1993)			
Table 2.1 UK exports to Japan	1993 $US'000	1990 $US'000	1985 $US'000
Medicinal and pharmaceutical goods	368,826	172,605	69,968
Road vehicles and parts	367,444	362,923	36,540
Office and data processing machinery	362,645	78,948	31,286
Miscellaneous manufacturers	294,327	793,148	106,434
Whisky and other beverages	233,415	292,493	93,034
Electrical machinery	187,896	213,756	78,496
Organic chemicals	160,357	145,163	110,357
Scientific and precision instruments	147,577	161,786	75,399
Non-ferrous metals	146,272	247,794	61,876
Transport equipment besides road vehicles	135,128	69,778	29,239
Total UK Exports to Japan	4,059,969	4,025,928	1,686,727

Source: The Anglo-Japanese Economic Institute, 1994, p.3.

Table 2.2 UK imports from Japan	1993 $US'000	1990 $US'000	1985 $US'000
Road vehicles and parts	3,038,859	2,244,782	1,321,292
Office and data processing machinery	1,868,752	1,437,578	752,405
Electrical machinery	1,847,084	1,340,997	776,236
Telecommunications and sound equipment	1,356,468	1,450,599	1,161,973
Miscellaneous manufacturers	960,561	562,499	416,522
Power generating machinery	709,341	373,316	133,807
General industrial machinery and parts	558,569	395,067	185,403
Photographic and optical goods; timepieces	401,984	405,121	294,563
Specialised industrial machinery	386,014	377,346	217,997
Scientific and precision instruments	296,767	210,407	110,017
Total UK Imports from Japan	13,060,303	10,345,235	6,299,046

Source: The Anglo-Japanese Economic Institute, 1994, p.3.

In general though, how much of the trade imbalance can be blamed on trade barriers restricting the flow of imports into Japan? Furthermore how much are conventional or formal trade barriers, such as tariffs and import quotas, to blame and how much comes down to informal barriers, including government red tape, complex import regulations, and structural economic factors beyond the control of central government? These questions have obviously been the focus of much debate in recent years because of Japan's huge trade surplus, particularly with the USA. The real causes and effects of Japan's alleged protectionism are difficult in practice to pinpoint and tend to get buried beneath the political rhetoric and posturing that accompanies international trade negotiations at the highest levels.

In theory a closed economy pays for its own protectionism in the form of higher consumer prices and higher costs of inputs into industry, resulting in a distorted domestic economy (and usually in an increased demand for cheaper imports - which would rapidly stabilise an open economy). The evidence suggests that this is precisely the case in Japan, with customers paying over the odds (80 percent over the OECD average) for goods and services that are cheaper in the West. Work in early 1995 by Japanese researchers (Sazanami et al., 1995) compares the price of imports on the dockside (before tariffs or distribution costs etc.. have been added) with the price of Japanese goods at the factory gate. The difference between these prices, for identical or similar goods, indicates how much Japanese customers are paying for both formal and informal trade barriers

(Economist, 1995).

The findings show that the heaviest protection is in agricultural products and some specific manufacturing industries. Top of the list is milled rice, followed by tea and coffee where local prices were over 700 percent higher than import prices. Japanese-made radios and televisions were over 600 percent more expensive than imports (although local models are acknowledged to be more advanced), clothing about 300 percent and petrol about 200 percent. As the formal import tariff rates for most of these products are low (for tea and coffee around 12 percent for radios and TVs zero percent, and for clothing about 10 percent) the researchers also conclude that non-tariff barriers are very high, at least in these sectors.

The total cost to Japanese consumers is estimated to be about 3.8 percent of GDP (in 1989), although if we discount the additional profits for domestic producers and the additional revenues for central government the cost is estimated at 0.6 percent of Japan's national income. Furthermore, as the data used for these estimates are from 1989 and as the Japanese yen has appreciated about 40 percent against the US dollar since then it is safe to assume that the overall cost to consumers is higher, as customers are not benefiting as much as they could from cheaper imports. Although the method by which these figures are arrived at and the validity of the data itself is debatable it is acknowledged by most economists that domestic costs are very high in Japan and informal barriers play a major role in closing out competition. The figures comparing Japan's inward and outward foreign direct investment tell the same story.

Foreign direct investment It is certain that constraints on FDI flows into Japan at least partly underlie the trade imbalance as a large proportion of imports are channelled via foreign firms with a local presence. Japan has the world's second largest economy but the lowest level of foreign investment per person of all the industrialised countries, $180. In Germany this figure is $800, in the US, $1,600, and in Britain a huge $2,000 worth of FDI per head of population. By March 1994 the total stock of FDI in Japan stood just under $30 billion and since 1950 42 percent has come from the USA, 29 percent from Europe and 5 percent from the UK. Japan's total FDI abroad totals $423 billion, giving it a ratio of outward to inward FDI of 14 to 1, compared to 1 to 1 in the UK, 1.1 to 1 in the USA and about 1.5 to 1 in Germany. In the UK it has invested over 22 times the amount that the UK has invested in Japan. Compared with other major economies, where 14 - 26 percent of industrial assets are controlled by foreigners, in Japan this proportion is 1 percent (Anglo-Japanese Economic Institute, 1994).

Table 2.3 compares Japan's ratio of FDI with each of its major trading partners, showing that the largest imbalance of FDI is with the UK.

The machinery sector ranks as the biggest foreign industry in Japan, in terms

Table 2.3 Japan's two-way direct overseas investments with leading industrial countries		
	Japan's direct investments, by country (US$m)	Foreign countries' direct investments in Japan (US$m)	Ratio of Japan's investment in host to host's investment in Japan
UK	31,661	1,403	22:1
Germany	7,334	1,357	5:1
France	5,974	598	10:1
Netherlands	18,397	2,277	8:1
Switzerland	3,128	1,995	2:1
USA	177,098	12,174	14:1
Total (all countries)	422,555	29,933	14:1

Source: The Anglo-Japanese Economic Institute, 1994, p.19.

of FDI and second is the chemicals and pharmaceuticals sector, which is the largest in terms of market share, capturing a quarter of the Japanese market (if we include drugs licensed to Japanese firms the proportion reaches 45 percent). Large and successful British companies like ICI, Zeneca and Glaxo are prominent in this latter sector. Table 2.4 provides a breakdown of FDI by industry sector.

When we look at the patterns of FDI in Japan over the last 10 or 15 years, several trends are worth noting. First, Europe overtook the USA in terms of the value and number of cases of investment from 1990 onwards, after being some way behind. Second, as regards FDI from all countries, manufacturing has declined steadily as a proportion of total FDI in Japan (not in terms of actual amounts, which have increased), from 70 percent in 1985 to just under 40 percent in 1992 in value and 60 percent to 22 percent in terms of the number of cases. This, and the rapid rise in the amount of Japanese FDI in manufacturing abroad (especially in Asia), has significant implications for the evolving structure of Japan's economy and foreign participation in various sectors.

A resurgence of Japanese foreign investment in the late 1980s meant that Japan regained its title as the world's largest holder of net foreign assets (US$383.1 billion at the end of 1991). Despite the fact that the value of the total stock of inward FDI in Japan at the end of 1989 was three times the value in 1980, two acquisitions, MCA by Matsushita ($6 billion) and Columbia Pictures by Sony ($3.4 billion)

Table 2.4   State of foreign direct investment in Japan by industry

	Total FDI for FY 1950-1992 (%)
Manufacturing	**56.9**
Foods	1.7
Textiles	0.3
Rubber/leather products	0.8
Chemicals	17.8
Petroleum	3.5
Glass/stone products	0.6
Metals	2.9
Machinery	27.1
Others	2.4
Non-manufacturing industries	**43.1**
Construction industry	0.4
Real estate industry	4.2
Trade and commerce	18.3
Service industry	9.0
Transportation	0.7
Communication	1.1
Banking and insurance	6.4
Others	3.0
Total	**100**

Source: JETRO, 1994a, p.6.

easily outweighed this increase.

Again there is evidence that the situation is beginning to change. Low profits have caused Japan's foreign direct investment abroad to fall by almost a half in the 4 years up to 1993 and with manufacturing FDI in Asia flourishing, Japanese investment in Europe and the USA is falling (Financial Times, 1995b). There has also been a noticeable turn-around in the ratio of acquisitions of foreign companies by Japanese against foreign acquisitions of Japanese companies. This is associated with the influx of overseas money into Japanese financial markets as foreign investors take advantage of low stock prices of Japanese companies. One recent report showed foreigners long-term investments in Japan having risen almost 40 percent, with money pouring into Japanese stocks and bonds to take advantage of the slump in the Japanese equity market. Another indication of the changing pattern of foreign involvement in the Japanese economy (Lawrence, 1992).

Foreign firms in Japan

It is estimated that there are something over 3,500 foreign and foreign-affiliated firms in Japan (including majority-owned joint-ventures), depending on the definitions used. On top of these there are many more companies registered in Japan but owned and operated by foreigners living there, plus numerous firms licensing, franchising and exporting to Japan via agents, that are not listed as foreign companies.

The foreign and foreign-affiliated firms in Japan employ up to 350,000 Japanese (Huddlestone, 1990). Beyond this, data on these firms, what they do, what proportion are SMEs, how they entered the local market and what local presence they maintain, is sketchy. But it is certain that they contribute to the flow of imports into the Japanese economy (hence the link between FDI and the trade balance).

By comparison to Japanese firms all foreign affiliates together account for a meagre 1.1 percent of local sales (2.5 percent in manufacturing). However, they do contribute 4.3 percent of all exports from Japan and a far more significant 16.2 percent of imports into the country (JETRO, 1995).

Around 400 of the total number of foreign firms in Japan are said to be British. Again, detailed figures have not been compiled but a significant proportion of exports to Japan enter via British firms that have established a presence in the local market. As it is the largest market for British firms outside Europe and North America these companies play an important role.

The figures vary considerably depending on the criteria used to define 'foreign'. By another definition, used by JETRO, 'foreign capitalised' companies in Japan number fewer than the above estimate and British companies comprise a lower proportion of the total (Table 2.5). Although the number of companies present bears no relation to the overall investment value it is interesting to note that the UK's proportion of total companies in Japan remained constant between 1985 and 1995.

Another study (this time by MITI) includes companies with over one-third equity owned by foreign nationals and estimated there were 1,486 of these in 1993. 74 percent were based in Tokyo, 8 percent in Osaka and 7 percent in Kanagawa. 45 percent were involved primarily in manufacturing, 40 percent in commerce and

9 percent in services. 43 percent were American and Western European countries accounted for 40 percent (JETRO, 1995).

Large firms, particularly the 25-30 Western companies in Japan with sales of over US$1billion, dominate the common foreign business knowledge about Japan. Amongst the largest UK firms with significant manufacturing and R&D investments in Japan are ICI, Glaxo, Unilever, Johnson Matthey, Amersham and English China Clays. Significantly, our understanding about the difficulties facing foreign firms trying to break in the Japanese market comes mainly from the press coverage of large firms' strategies and problems. They are used as illustrative case-studies by commentators and cited by politicians in negotiations with Japanese authorities when trying to improve access to domestic markets. The independent route taken by Toys-R-Us, for example, bypassing the established distribution and retail hierarchy and setting up its own discount outlets is legendary in Japan (Japan Times, 1994). Similarly, the stories of Rover and BMW are well-known management case-studies used to encourage aspiring entrants to take the independent route.

There has also been widespread discussion of the entry strategy followed by the German engineering group Bosch, which quietly developed links within the relevant *keiretsu* groups: via a Toyota affiliate Nippon Denso (in which it holds shares); via a joint venture with Mitsubishi Electric; and through part-ownership of Japan Electronic Control Systems, tied to Nissan. An approach

Table 2.5 Foreign-capitalized companies in Japan by country of origin and by year

	1985	1995
USA	720	1263
Canada	26	41
Austria	4	5
Belgium	10	26
Bulgaria	1	1
Czech	0	1
Denmark	16	33
Finland	17	17
France	105	202
Germany	185	300
Greece	0	1
Hungary	0	1
Ireland	2	6
Italy	25	50
Liechtenstein	2	6
Luxembourg	7	10
Netherlands	54	107
Norway	3	7
Poland	1	1
Portugal	1	1
Russia	1	1
Spain	4	9
Sweden	4	55
Switzerland	99	168
U.K.	143	259
Total	1430	2571

Source: Ministry of Finance statistics and JETRO (1995)

which contrasted the strategy followed by US motor parts makers who publicly lobbied their government to push for 'fair' access into Japan's auto industry on their behalf. Similarly, Merck's take over of Japan's drugs company Banyu, as Japan's biggest foreign takeover was fully covered by the financial press.

Recent illustrations of the growing opportunities for foreign firms in Japan include the trade figures for the high-profile car and car components sectors. While US and Japanese policy makers continued to disagree on the setting of quantifiable levels of imports into Japan the high yen promoted the incursion of US car firms into the Japanese market. General Motors more than doubled car registrations in Japan in 1993 and Ford boosted its sales by 50 percent. Greater price competitiveness and customer acceptance also helped Chrysler win a four-fold increase in registrations in Japan. Similarly, Japanese producers purchased more and more imported car parts in attempts to keep their own costs down. In 1993 Toyota increased its purchases of US car components by 5 percent over the previous year and now spends about 4 times the amount it spent 5 years ago on imported parts (Nakamoto, 1994b).

Another example is beer. Beer imports into Japan increased five-fold in the first 4 months of 1994, helped by the efforts of discount retailers who are increasingly cutting out the wholesalers and middlemen in an effort to undercut the powerful influence of the four dominant domestic brewers (Terazono, 1994c).

But while both examples show the growth in market opportunities for foreign firms in Japan they can also be used to demonstrate the resilience of some Japanese market barriers to foreign competition. Foreign beers, for example, still only have two percent of the Japanese market, despite the fact that they are up to half the price of local brands. Likewise, imports make up just 8 percent of Japan's spirits market compared to an average of 30 percent across other OECD countries. This is partly because imports, like Scotch Whisky are taxed up to 6 times as much as local brands like Shochu (with 67 percent of the market) (Abrahams, 1994). Similarly, despite the impressive figures for increased imports of foreign cars, Japan imported just 3 percent of its cars and 2 percent of its car parts last year. For the other OECD countries comparable proportions for cars range from 22 percent to 78 percent and from 16 percent to 60 percent for car parts (Nakamoto and Abrahams, 1994).

The same imbalance can be found in other sectors. Japan's insurance market and the telecommunications industry, both of which are the second largest in the world, are also the focus of trade-lobbyists attention. Foreign firms have only 2 percent of Japan's insurance market, compared to between 10 percent and 34 percent in other G7 countries. The country also imports just 5 percent of its telecoms equipment (in 1991), compared to an average of 25 percent in other G7 countries (28 percent in the USA) (Nakamoto and Abrahams, 1994).

British SMEs in Japan

Comprehensive data relating firm size with FDI in Japan and trade with Japan is not available so it is not known precisely what proportion of Britain's trade with Japan comes from SMEs. However, the prominence of such firms in both the British and the Japanese economies and the degree to which trade is channelled via foreign firms abroad suggests their role is significant.

In the UK an estimated 64 percent of firms employ less than 500 people (the OECD SME definition) and about 2 million UK 'small' businesses (employing less than 200 employees) account for 75 percent of the workforce. In Japan a slightly different definition of SME is used, depending on the sector. In manufacturing SMEs are defined as having fewer than 300 employees or less than 100 million Yen capitalisation value; in wholesaling the limit is 100 employees (30 million Yen); and in retailing and services it is fewer than 50 employees (10 million Yen). A separate category of 'small-scale enterprises' is defined as fewer than 20 employees in manufacturing and less than 5 in commerce and services. 73 percent of firms are SMEs (*chu-sho kigyo*) and almost 50 percent of the workforce is employed in firms of less than 100 people (Japan Small Business Corporation, 1993; Sengenberger et al. 1989).

Of the estimated 400 British firms in Japan (numbers vary widely according to definitions of ownership, control and capitalization) probably just under half are SMEs. There are some indications that a relatively higher number of British SMEs have successfully established themselves in Japan compared to other European investors (although Asian investors tend to be the smallest). The clearest illustration is the difference between (1) Britain's proportion of total cumulative FDI in Japan compared to that of other countries (5 percent, counting all FDI flows from 1950 to 1992) and (2) Britain's share of the total number of cases of FDI (individual investments) in the same time period (8.7 percent). This suggests that the total value of British investments have been spread across a comparatively large number of smaller enterprises. The equivalent proportions for the USA are 41.9 percent and 19 percent showing that its large volume of cumulative FDI has been spread across relatively fewer larger firms (particularly the car companies, and affiliates of large IT companies) (JETRO, 1994a).

Data that gives the average value of FDI per case show which sectors tend to be dominated by small firms and which by larger firms. Just taking manufacturing FDI into Japan the chemicals sector, rubber and leather products and, predictably, petroleum are all dominated by larger investors. The machinery sector, metals, 'spun and woven products' and foods are all sectors where SMEs are responsible for relatively more FDI into Japan.

Why Japan?

As stated in this book's introduction, the clearest single message that comes from those that have a long experience of managing businesses in Japan is that the Japanese market needs long-term commitment. This is not, perhaps, a particularly new message. Its reputation as a tough market, sometimes as an entirely closed market has been so well emphasised as to discourage many potential entrants. Despite this the actual reasons underlying the need for long-term commitment are not clearly understood by those that are new to Japan.

What makes the Japanese market require this extra commitment? What makes the Japanese market *deserve* extra commitment? The next two chapters will examine this first question, describing the experiences of the British SMEs that provided case studies for this book. Here we will provide a brief answer to the second question, outlining the main reasons why firms that are successfully doing business with Japan were attracted to its markets in the first place.

The answer is relatively straightforward in that the main attraction to Japan for foreign firms is the 'bottom line' ie. profits, through access to the large and lucrative Japanese market. Profits of foreign affiliates in Japan have always been, on average, higher than those of local Japanese firms. Although data is imprecise estimates suggest that in the late 1980s (before the high-yen recession) profits of foreign affiliates in Japan, as a percentage of gross sales, averaged 3.8 percent (and 4.6 percent in manufacturing), compared to 2.3 percent (3.4 percent in manufacturing) for Japanese firms. Relative to local firms foreign firms' profits are notably high in electrical machinery and manufacturing (excluding petroleum) but lower than Japanese firms in general machinery, transport machinery and chemicals and pharmaceuticals (March, 1990). In 1992 these figures were significantly lower, with profits averaging 3.0 percent (3.3 percent in manufacturing) for foreign firms. But the gap in profit rates compared with Japanese firms (1.8 percent and 2.6 percent respectively) still remained (JETRO, 1994b). These percentages, combined with the very large size of Japan's domestic market (second only to the USA) provide the clearest rationale for most foreign firms. For most of these firms success in Japan means high revenues and good profits. For some this is their one and only market and for many others the Japanese operations represent a significant proportion of their overall activities and income.

There are additional benefits associated with maintaining a direct presence in Japan, rather than exporting via an agent or distributor, which are discussed in the following chapters. For companies bringing in goods and services for sale to Japanese consumers or a sub-contractors to Japanese companies, a local presence allows direct contact with customers. This is essential for product adaptation, customization and development specifically for the Japanese market, and for provision of technical maintenance and after-sales support services.

In specific sectors, notably autos, consumer electronics and construction, foreign companies have established a base in Japan to get access to Japanese business abroad, particularly as many purchasing decisions are made at company HQ in Japan and buyer-supplier relationships are best developed with head office staff. Japan also provides a secondary access for many firms to the rapidly growing markets of S.E.Asia and China, either through Japanese firms, as sub-contractors and suppliers to Japanese plants being set up in cheap labour areas, or on the back of growing Japanese trade with the newly industrialised countries (NICs).

Foreign companies have also listed 'learning effects' as one of the main benefits derived from exposure to Japan's competitive market environment. In most cases improvements in manufacturing efficiency or customer service, for example, gained from the experience of working for Japanese companies or trying to please Japanese consumers, were important benefits but not the primary reason for locating in Japan. In other cases, particularly in high-technology areas and in industry sectors where Japanese firms were at the forefront of new technologies or led the world in new product development, foreign companies emphasised the strategic need to be close to the best, in Japan. In the next part of this book there are a number of examples of how companies improved aspects of their competitiveness by learning from Japan.

This answers the question of why some companies see Japan's markets as deserving the extra investment, effort, commitment and understanding required to sell products or establish a business presence. It does not answer the question of whether the cost-benefit balance is right for any individual firm thinking about getting into Japan. As with all investment decisions this is difficult because of the natural uncertainty and inherent risk involved in assessing potential future rewards and the price of attaining them. The next chapters of this book look at the experience of British SMEs who have succeeded in Japan and derive lessons for companies who are attracted to Japan but need to know more about what costs and benefits to expect. For those that have made the decision to invest in Japan, the following illustrates how others have prepared for, adapted to and developed businesses in Japan, in the belief that, just as knowledge reduces uncertainty, a more informed approach is more likely to lead to success.

3 Getting into the Japanese market

Returning now to the central theme of this book, the survey of UK SMEs in Japan, the following sections will review the main insights gained from the interviews in British firms already experiencing some success in Japan. How did they establish themselves in Japan? What problems did they encounter? Did they receive useful support from the British or Japanese government trade promotion agencies? And once there, what are the main difficulties associated with managing Japanese employees, maintaining links with UK headquarters or adapting products for the domestic Japanese market? Also, how have these firms benefited from their exposure to Japan's competitive market and its demanding customers? Have they learnt first-hand from the manufacturing prowess or product development skills of their local competitors? Has their experience in Japan contributed to improvements in the production, management, marketing or other business processes in their organisations as a whole?

Part (A) will examine how the UK SMEs studied first entered the Japanese market, how they financed their investment and the problems they encountered. Part (B) focuses on one of the most critical factors of success, an understanding of customer requirements in Japan and the development good supplier-buyer relationships. Part (C) then reviews the type of assistance the survey firms received from the various government agencies that exist in Britain and Japan to provide support for new entrants into Japan (and looks at what is available now). Chapter 4 will then focus on the main problems experienced by British SMEs once in Japan, how they overcame these and what they learnt in the process. (Some of the case study material is described in more detail in example 'boxes' in the following pages, to illustrate key points).

Entering the market: common routes and problems

Some of the main insights into British SME operations in Japan from this survey will be described in the following sections based on the project's original 'Terms of Reference'. It will look at: (i) the main ways of establishing a base in Japan, depending on the type of firm and its market objectives, and list some key points for a successful initial start in Japan; (ii) how SMEs tend to finance their presence in Japan, and; (iii) the importance of long-term commitment from the UK-end of the business to the Japanese operation.

Establishing a base in Japan: why do it and how to do it?

Why and how the sample firms initially established a base in Japan varies considerably according to the size, sector and structure of their overall companies. In most cases, however, the key factor was the perceived market for their products and services in Japan and, often, the envisaged growth potential for this market. In some cases, particularly the construction sector, the main objective was to get close to Japanese companies involved in projects in third countries, as co-suppliers or partners. By setting up an office in Japan these firms network directly with senior Japanese decision-makers at company headquarters and can pitch for project work quickly and accurately. For a range of British firms established in Japan the local office also had a role in monitoring new products and technologies emerging from Japanese competitors to inform decision-makers in the UK. Increasingly, in addition to the above reasons, companies aimed to use Japan as a base for entering into the expanding Asian market.

The entry route is decided during the initial exploratory phase when firms identify the existence, size and characteristics of their market in Japan. Despite the importance of this phase many firms had, in retrospect, been reactive rather than proactive in their approach to the Japanese market and many admitted they had failed to carry out adequate research on their Japanese consumers, competitors and partners in preparation. Indecision in many cases had led to a lack of early commitment and a lack of investment in the early stages which, with hindsight, had proved to be more damaging in Japan than would be the case in other markets. Many firms reported early difficulties with Japanese distributors, sales and marketing agents, again mainly because of a lack of understanding of the differences in Japanese practices. But managers also complained of the difficulties of getting reliable information on potential markets and Japanese partners.

A significant number of firms included in this survey (about a quarter) had already developed some ties with Japanese buyers before establishing themselves in Japan. Many had sold indirectly, through a trading company, or via a larger

British firm already based in Japan. Others had created links with Japanese companies in Europe. Those involved in the construction industry in particular had usually carried out sub-contracting work for large Japanese companies in third country projects and were strengthening ties and improving their chances of winning further work by placing themselves near a major source of business, ie. the headquarters of some of the world's largest construction and engineering firms. They also had hopes for an accelerated opening up of the notoriously closed domestic construction market in Japan and some were already experiencing success in particular local niches.

These initial links with Japanese companies or Japan's domestic market (even, in one case, a senior manager's holiday in Japan) had started many firms along a learning curve, characterised by a growing interest in the business opportunities in Japan and a growing understanding of how the firm would need to adapt to grasp these opportunities. On the one hand this represents a natural and secure route for company expansion, particularly by SMEs that do not have the resources to investigate new markets and tend to be responsive to new opportunities only where they arise directly from existing activities. On the other hand, however, across all the firms surveyed (all of which are now competing successfully in Japan) it was surprising to note how often the very first contact or spark of interest had occurred purely by chance. Very few firms had proactively sought out opportunities for their products and services in one of the biggest domestic markets in the global economy. Our view is that this stems not from any lack of entrepreneurial spirit amongst small companies, but from Japan's over-exaggerated reputation as an impenetrable, expensive marketplace.

It should be said that a common factor amongst many of the firms studied, and one that perhaps separates them from the 'average' SME, is that once the initial link had been made and the first order had come from a Japanese buyer, a big effort was made to meet and even exceed the requirements set by the new business partner. It was this initial effort, and the insight and determination not to treat the Japanese buyer like any other buyer that underlay this effort, and enabled the development of a longer-term business relationship

Before examining start-up routes taken by British SMEs in Japan we can look at two comparative studies from the USA (although variable definitions make comparisons difficult). The first, a US Department of Commerce study, found that 70 percent of investment in foreign firms in Japan established since 1973 had been in 100 percent-owned subsidiaries (due partly to changes in the foreign investment laws in 1972). But it also found that 60 percent of foreign direct investment in manufacturing had been in joint-ventures. The findings of the second study are listed on Table (3.1), which also gives an indication of which routes are favoured by different sectors (Lawrence, 1992).

Table 3.1   Majority-owned foreign direct investment in Japan: percentage of firms, by industry and method of entry, 1991

Industry	(a)	(b)	(c)	Number of firms that responded
Total Investment	**43.7**	**49.3**	**07.1**	**1,234**
Manufacturing	**51.0**	**40.3**	**08.7**	**576**
-Manufacturing except oil	51.1	40.7	08.2	562
-Food processing	52.4	33.3	14.3	21
-Textiles	57.1	42.9	00.0	7
-Wood products	42.9	57.1	00.0	7
-Pulp and paper	20.0	80.0	00.0	5
-Publishing and printing	33.3	6.7	00.0	12
-Chemicals	62.3	29.8	07.9	114
-Pharmaceuticals	44.4	44.4	11.1	45
-Oil	50.0	21.4	28.6	14
-Rubber	50.0	41.7	08.3	12
-Leather	50.0	50.0	00.0	2
-Clay and ceramics	50.0	50.0	00.0	14
-Steel and Iron	00.0	00.0	00.0	0
-Non-ferrous metals	35.7	50.0	14.3	14
-Processed Steel	40.0	50.0	10.0	10
-General machinery	52.4	37.8	09.8	82
-Electric machinery	50.5	45.9	03.7	109
-Transportation machinery	59.1	22.7	18.2	22
-Precision machinery	38.3	51.7	10.0	60
-Weapons	00.0	00.0	00.0	0
-Other manufactured	61.5	26.9	11.5	26
Commerce	**38.0**	**56.0**	**06.0**	**502**
Oil Sales	**00.0**	**00.0**	**00.0**	**0**
Services	**34.3**	**61.1**	**04.6**	**108**
Other	**35.4**	**60.4**	**04.2**	**48**
Oil related services	**50.0**	**21.4**	**28.6**	**14**

(a)   **Creation of joint venture**
(b)   **Creation of new company (Greenfield)**
(c)   **Capital participation (M&A activity)**

Source: Lawrence, 1992, p.65.

Our sample can be divided into 4 broad groups according to the way they first entered the market: 'local entrepreneurial start-ups' (6 of the 30, representing all but one of the 7 independent KKs); 'arms-length entrants' (10); 'joint ventures' (6); and 'cold or standing starts' (8).

Local entrepreneurial start-ups Predictably there was a major contrast between the small independent KKs and the other sample firms which were headquartered in the UK or part of a larger corporate group. The former tended to be established by entrepreneurs who had already gained considerable experience in Japan, often with larger British companies and had taken the opportunity to set up their own business. The network of customers and contacts already known to these owner-managers was a central factor in their success.

The process of setting up an independent company (a *Yugen Kaisha*, YK, or KK) is relatively straightforward given that these managers usually know the language and the relevant government regulations, have had time to research the market 'in-situ', are used to working with Japanese employees, and have an existing support network. Their reasons for branching out on their own are generally a mixture of personal objectives and perceived business opportunities. Several individuals had established themselves with the help of a Japanese spouse, who could provide local contacts, credibility (stability and reputation) and, as Japanese nationals, access to local sources of finance and relevant trading permits.

Although many of these companies had funding sources and/or personal bases in the UK (houses or family etc..) they tended to be committed to a long-term association with Japan on an independent personal and professional basis. As such their start-up process could be termed the most entrepreneurial because of the high levels of risk involved. Moreover, their insights into the problems of working and succeeding in Japan, having seen many colleagues and friends fail, were often the most in-depth.

Arms-length entrants Amongst the UK-based SMEs surveyed there was a substantial variation in the reasons for wanting to set up a permanent presence in Japan and in the market entry mechanisms adopted. Many had begun by exporting products at 'arms-length' via a Japanese distributor or trading company and had then decided at a later stage that the market warranted a greater degree of involvement and investment. For a large number of firms that had started this way dissatisfaction with the marketing or distribution efforts of Japanese partners had led to the decision to base in-house representatives in Japan. In these cases companies wanted to develop more first-hand knowledge of their market in Japan through more direct interaction with customers, believing they could serve their markets better than Japanese representatives. In other cases an expanding market justified additional local investment. Companies were satisfied at the markets reached via their Japanese representatives (treating the initial phase as a test period) and sought to expand sales activities.

The *sogo shosha* trading companies are the best-known route for exporting to Japan, but not necessarily the best. British managers with some of bringing in goods to Japan suggest the *senmon shosha*, the numerous (over 10,000), smaller, more specialised distributers, are often more effective. These are particularly useful for small volume sales and for specialised or customised goods needing technical expertise and a closer customer link. It is, however, more difficult for a newcomer to Japan to search and select the most suitable for a particular product because *senmon shosha* vary enormously in size and market coverage, and in terms of technical and marketing ability.

Many of the sample firms were involved in capital goods manufacturing, some in fairly high-technology products (such as measuring instruments). For most firms, but particularly these, market expansion meant there was also a growing need for technical support and/or after-sales service to be developed alongside product sales, requiring a greater degree of interaction between customers and themselves. The need to further adapt products in various ways for the Japanese market was also a common reason for establishing a permanent presence. In both cases a Japan office provided the infrastructure for technical know-how and troubleshooting support to flow from producer to customer (and back), either via expatriate technicians or through permanent local employees with a direct allegiance to the British producer rather than the distributor. Although Japanese partners can (and do) provide technical and after-sales support for foreign firms it proved too difficult for the majority of firms sampled to develop their existing relationship to fulfil this role, often because the Japanese partner was not capable or not willing to develop a specialist technical support function in addition to marketing, sales and distribution activities.

A key problem for firms that took the arms-length entry route was finding an appropriate distributor or marketing agent with experience of the product and the market but without an existing competitor product. Dissatisfaction with the marketing efforts of the Japanese partner was a common problem, often linked to a lack of first-hand experience on the UK-side regarding the Japanese customer and the styles of marketing that are acceptable or effective in Japan. Further problems appeared at the point when the SME broke off its original link to establish its own presence. Transferring customer ties to a new entity and establishing new lines of distribution and sales support are notoriously difficult in Japan. It was noticeable that the more successful British firms tended to be the ones that had 'taken on' (poached) staff from the Japanese partner to bring in local experience, retain customers and encourage other suitable Japanese employees to work in the new office.

Joint ventures In some cases the relationships between British firms and Japanese distributors or sales agents described above were set up as formal joint ventures, with co-ownership. But 6 other firms started in Japan as 'true' joint ventures with a Japanese parent, wherein the latter either co-manufactured the product with the UK-side or manufactured similar products independently. Very often these were formed in high-technology sectors, such as industrial pumps, power supplies and electrical systems (Figure 1.1), where the firms were sub-contracting to large Japanese firms. Factors such as the high costs of entering these markets, the need for immediate, on-site technical support and the value customers place on long-term supplier ties and trusted engineering back-up all made close local market partnerships necessary. In return the British companies tended to be offering niche products, new technology and/or a global reputation for high quality (even global leadership) in a very specific area. Rarely were they given access solely on the basis of low prices, although price has been an increasingly important factor for Japanese buyers in the 1990s

   In all but one of the sample firms the joint venture had ended following a rift between the parent companies. In most cases problems arise over the control of the joint venture and its development. Very often the UK-side initiated the break-up after it found it had less control over the venture and less access to final customers than anticipated, mainly because the company was staffed by employees loyal to the Japanese parent.

   In one notable case the partners' relationship had evolved from that of cooperative co-producers to that of adversarial competitors. The UK parent then managed something of a coup together with the Japanese managers of the joint venture (originally senior employees of the Japanese parent company) by setting up a rival (wholly-owned) subsidiary company with 23 poached employees while simultaneously selling off all shares in the joint venture to the Japanese parent. Despite this aggressive move the latter surprisingly still retained a role established before the joint venture as the main distributor for a range of other products from the UK parent.

   A chemicals company examined had experienced a very different partnership. Having begun as a branch office it entered into a joint venture with a major Japanese player with plans to share production technology and invest in a local manufacturing facility. After extensive discussion the expansion plans were eventually shelved by the Japanese side leading to the collapse of the joint venture. The company reverted to its branch office status with a Japanese President who, with hindsight, blamed the failure on the poor choice of Japanese partner made by inexperienced British expatriate managers who had been in charge of the original branch office.

A final example is an industrial pump manufacturer that entered Japan via a joint venture focused on adapting specific products for Japanese corporate customers. As the market expanded, the distribution and technical support capabilities of the jointly-owned company proved too small and tension in the relationship increased as the Japanese side refused to invest or provide additional support for the operation. Moreover, as the joint venture was managed by secondees from the Japanese parent it began increasingly to pull away from UK control. This resulted in a protracted takeover battle with the UK side eventually buying out the Japanese parent but facing major problems trying to retain key staff and maintain local customers.

Although these joint venture experiences look fairly negative most of the managers involved still believed that they had gained considerable benefits from the close tie-up with an experienced Japanese company in their field and see it as their best option as a market entry strategy. With hindsight managers would have prepared more effectively for the break-up of the arrangement by learning more from their Japanese partners and entering into direct contact with customers at an earlier stage.

Many problems are said to arise from a rushed search and selection process leading to 'shotgun partnerships' where a poor match leaves both sides dissatisfied. It is often pressure from headoffice in UK forcing the timing for market entry into Japan, without an understanding of the importance of research and preparation, that creates this problem. Common advice for British firms looking to enter into joint ventures, beyond 'take your time', include:

- have a definite product, technology or brand to provide immediate focus and a source of profit for both sides, to 'kick-start' the venture;

- understand fully the objectives and expectations of the Japanese side regarding the partnership as any miscommunication at the initial stage will cause serious difficulties (usually for the foreign company) later;

- be prepared for a relatively long initial payout period (try not to push the Japanese partner into producing returns at an early stage in the venture);

- understand that the Japanese side is likely to be expecting a long-term relationship, as it has with suppliers and distributors and other local firms, rather than a short-term arrangement.

Despite the many difficulties (and some of the horror stories) joint ventures are still one of the commonest routes into Japan because they allow the foreign partner to plug into the networks, distribution channels and experience of the Japanese company, therefore bypassing many of the initial difficulties that can defeat other firms. The key lesson is to use the joint venture as a platform for learning about Japan, creating independent networks and making contact with your customers, ready for self-sufficiency.

'Cold' or 'standing' start This involves setting up a permanent presence in Japan from the outset in the case of companies who are confident of their market and/ or have products or services that cannot be sold through an intermediary. Sample firms that followed this route often had to carry out a considerable amount of product adaptation or full-scale manufacturing from the start, as in the case of the paper products manufacturer where transport costs of bulk raw materials unusually made it economic to manufacture the product in Japan. On the whole, however, this route is more characteristic of large firms, such as Rover and Toys-R-US, that can afford the high levels of investment required to by-pass local distribution systems and other existing networks, rather than SMEs.

Other sample firms had entirely different reasons for placing in-house representatives in Japan from the beginning. In some cases there was a need to get close to existing Japanese clients who were already served in other markets. For example, two firms that had acted as sub-contractors for Japanese multinationals in other global markets (one in the UK construction industry) had set up small liaison offices to make direct links with purchasing departments and decision-makers at local company headquarters to boost the number of contracts placed through their companies abroad.

According to the interviewees the obvious lesson for establishing a local presence without having 'tested the water', particularly if your firm does not have the financial muscle and the high market profile of some larger firms, is to prepare the ground thoroughly before making the investment. There is no substitute for senior managers personally researching the pitfalls of setting up an office and developing an understanding of their Japanese market and how business in their sector is conducted.

Key points for a successful entry

A general 'rule' emphasised by the managers interviewed on the subject of getting into the Japanese market was that no matter how good your product was and how well it sold in other markets you cannot 'just walk in' and do business in Japan. This may apply to new markets anywhere but in Japan it appears to be doubly important. Preparation is everything, and this has to go beyond information-gathering on markets and competitors, start-up costs and Government investment regulations. Learning the language is very useful but personal contacts are essential. Foreign managers must learn in some detail the inter-firm and inter-organisation networks relevant to their particular areas of business. They must know which trade and industry bodies act as a focus for which kinds of business activity, both government-related and private. They must establish which of their local competitors are allied with which supplier networks, retailers, banks, and so on and know how their market entry is likely to be received by these groups. It is even useful to know the particular affiliations of any consultant or advisor hired to help in the market-entry process. In some cases this is not even to give your company the competitive 'edge' but just a starting point for doing business successfully. If it is not already clear, further case-study examples in Chapter 4, looking at the problems of managing in Japan, should make it obvious why certain steps are necessary.

As described earlier in this book, these kinds of business relationships are far more closely knit in Japan compared to the UK or most other economies. New entrants or changes in business activity are very noticeable to local companies (and distributors, retailers and public-sector agencies) and efficient managerial grapevines between companies in similar or connecting sectors often exist for disseminating relevant news and coordinating unified responses. In many (not all) sectors this high level of interactivity and the form of 'cooperative competition' allows Japanese firms to 'accommodate' or 'exclude' newcomers very effectively.

In some ways all of these issues come under the general heading of 'adaptation'. Experienced managers emphasise that when foreign firms begin to operate in the home ground of the Japanese they need to learn about the Japanese way of doing business and quickly adapt to it. A big part of this involves changes in the management and organisation of local employees, as well as changes to products and services (discussed later in this chapter).

Getting good local advisors, whether Japanese or experienced expatriate managers, to help in the initial set-up was also stressed by recent entrants. Some mentioned lawyers, bankers or senior managers from local joint venture partners, with experience in a particular aspect of the business, a degree of local respect and a range of local contacts. Hiring senior Japanese managers with experience of working in the target market may be difficult but will help to manoeuvre the company into the relevant business networks. Most foreign firms in Japan either start with, or evolve towards a Japanese managing director or 'president' because this is essential for the close business relationships necessary to succeed in local markets as well as for internal organisational stability. Selecting the right person for this position is a critical element of success.

The careful selection of an appropriate entry mechanism is also important. With Japan there is arguably a greater degree of 'lock-in' to the first entry route selected (whether at arms-length via a supplier, or through a joint-venture, etc..), and less margin for error or flexibility to change strategies, than in other overseas markets. This is partly because corporate image and reputation are so strongly emphasised and customers (as well as other affiliated companies, service providers and financiers, etc..) tend to respect and trust stability and commitment to business relationships once they are forged. Shifting alliances early in the process of establishing a business in Japan rings alarm bells in local firms.

Overall it appears that in Japan there are no (or far fewer) second chances at making a 'first impression'. Overwhelmingly the advice to newcomers to Japan is to take time to invest in learning about the local people, companies, organisations and networks that relate to their area of business and invest in establishing a stable 'presence' for customers and local firms to recognise and respect.

Financing a presence in Japan

Japan is expensive place to live and work and an expensive place to establish a business. Chapter 4 gives some specific examples of the costs of starting up and running a company office in Japan. The following section will look at some of the ways that UK SMEs finance their initial investment and maintain a degree of financial security in Japan.

A recent survey from the UK's Institute of Export shows that most British firms finance their exports using working capital, usually their bank overdraft. Only 5 percent use their own funds. The survey suggests that this partly reflects the decline in special export finance schemes available from British banks (these fell from 13 to 5 in 1992-1993, key years for many of the firms surveyed)(Batchelor, 1993). British SMEs with a presence in Japan, most of which are importers into Japan, generally follow this pattern of financing.

Variations across the sample SMEs were due mainly to differences in ownership and local status, ties with head office and with UK banks, length of time in Japan and access to Japanese 'guarantors'. Most of the independent KK firms were funded 'in-house' either by personal savings, personal loans or private shareholder capital, sometimes from Japanese 'directors' or other local financiers.

4 of the 7 independent KKs were married to Japanese and could get access to local bank loans by using them as guarantors and in some cases by using local property as collateral.

For branches and subsidiaries funding differences hinged on the degree to which the Japan operation had been established as an offshoot of the parent, using capital investments from central company funds, or an independent profit-and-loss centre with financial autonomy. Some companies had moved from the former to the latter, giving the offshoot time to get established in appropriate markets and gain credibility with Japanese banks and investors before 'cutting the cord'.

Bank loans from UK banks are only possible if a subsidiary can get support and guarantees from its HQ in Britain. If they are given the backing of a creditable firm at home subsidiaries in Japan can get funding much the same way and on the same terms as if a British company in Britain took out a loan. However, many HQs prefer subsidiaries to be financially autonomous and subsidiaries very often do not want to be answerable to HQ for detailed expenditure and investments.

In general the message from the managers was that Japanese banks will not willingly lend to foreigners, especially not SMEs, especially not newcomers. This is partly to do with the traditional position of banks in the Japanese economy. Most commercial banks belong to *keiretsu* groups of companies in a paternal network where they exert a significant influence via loans and share mechanisms. Banks tend to avoid dealing with firms that are outside this network, including new Japanese firms that do not have a stamp of approval from known corporations or powerful local individuals. This reticence has worsened following the financial instabilities caused by the collapse of the property market which left many banks weak and risk averse. One of the main advantages of entering into a joint venture with a Japanese company is that this provides access to the partner's sources of local finance. Moreover, if the split is handled amicably, the Japanese parent may be willing to act as a guarantor for further loans to the UK firm's subsidiary in Japan.

An SME's chances of borrowing from local banks are improved if it has been in Japan for several years, and if it is KK-registered and has gained credibility with customers and other Japanese firms. Also beneficial is if a company has received funding or loans from a government source, such as the Ministry of Trade and Industry (MITI) or a regional development agency. This gives an additional 'stamp of approval'. Five companies out of the sample had received loan assistance from Japanese government sources (discussed later in this chapter).

One subsidiary, previously supported by finance from the UK, backed from company headquarters, received an £850,000 loan from the Japan Development Bank, through the Bank of Tokyo. This removed the debt burden from the UK HQ and made the subsidiary financially autonomous and in a much better position to negotiate local commercial loans in the future. The loan did not require collateral or mortgage backing and, as is traditional in Japan, the central guarantee was the personal *hanko* (a carved stamp of an individual's or company's initials which acts as a binding signature in Japan) of the Japanese president of the subsidiary, as a show of commitment to the regulations governing the loan. The personal risk for this president was partly offset by a letter of release from the loan regulations provided by the company. But should there be any problems with repayment this individual could be held personally responsible and stands to lose a great deal, which is enough to dissuade many managers from entering into such agreements.

On the whole the sample companies tended to be reticent about giving financial details, particularly stipulating costs, loans, debt and so on in actual figures. But one company provides an example of the sources and levels of financing generally used by SMEs in Japan. The Japan branch of a UK-based engineering and consultancy firm in the construction business with about 10 employees began with about £25,000 start up capital direct from headquarters plus various bank loans and a 'MEGS' (Market Entry Guarantee Scheme, coordinated by the DTI) loan worth £30,000 each year for three years. These all helped keep the main branch overdraft to around £100,000 in the early days.

In addition to the lack of credit for foreign companies and SMEs in Japan many companies complained of the high costs and unnecessary complications involved in the provision of international banking services and transactions by Japanese banks. Domestic commercial banks in Japan, despite being related to the largest international banks in the world, are relatively unsophisticated when it comes to money transfers to and from abroad, foreign exchange services and trade-related finance. International banks in Japan, who specialise in such services on a global scale, tend to be only interested in assisting large firms.

There are a number of exceptions. Tokyo Soya Bank, according to several interviewees, gave active encouragement to foreign SMEs in Japan, with bilingual staff and a range of schemes to handle international accounts and SME loans. National Westminster had also attempted to set up an advisory support service for foreign SMEs in Japan but had failed to make it economic and closed down after three years of trying.

Letters of credit and the system of promissory notes for supplier-buyer transactions were specifically mentioned by managers as examples of how local banks added to the high start-up costs and debt problems of foreign SMEs during their early period in Japan. The promissory notes system delays payments from buyers by about 6 months, representing a significant period of outstanding credit, which the bank will often not discount. Letters of credit are usually required for non-domestic transactions if a company is new to Japan. For example, if a branch office places an international order from its UK headquarters to buy from a

Japanese company a letter of credit is required with the order to guarantee final payment. This legally ties up a certain amount of finance until delivery of the goods (60 days or so) and also makes it difficult to change the order at a later date. Letters of credit were described as costly and inflexible by one interviewee, as well as demonstrating a certain lack of trust of outsiders.

In some cases successful entry into Japan will be entirely dependent on the investment funds available. Finance is often the 'bottom line', and the bottom line about Japan is that it is expensive and for many foreign companies, particularly SMEs, it is difficult to get finance locally. Most managers in the smaller firms interviewed for this survey had apocryphal stories about entry failures and debt-laden firms where good products or entrepreneurial ideas had failed to take off because managers underestimated the sheer cost of doing business in Japan.

Preparation and commitment from the UK

When we consider the firms that are linked to some degree to UK-based operations (over two-thirds of the sample), either as branches or locally registered but with a UK headoffice, those with the highest levels of commitment from home-base tended to be the most successful in Japan. In many cases the initial interest in Japanese markets came from senior board members or (often in smaller SMEs or those led by a strong entrepreneur) from the managing director. These influential decision-makers saw entry into Japan as a central management priority and were willing to invest personal time and company money to understand the market and establish a long-term presence there.

Senior-level commitment tends to follow from an understanding of the market and the belief in the opportunities it offers amongst senior managers. This not only reaffirms a company's decision to invest in Japan and place the best managers available to lead the Japan operation but also facilitates the various adaptations at home in management and products required to make a success of this investment. Companies that saw Japan as just another Asian market amongst many and lumped the region in with other Asian ventures did not tend to give sufficient support for the added investment needed, did not provide sufficient autonomy for their subsidiary to cope with the differences in Japan or back the required changes at UK production bases and head office.

An important thing to recognise is that Japanese customers, sub-contractors, banks, distributor companies, other local firms and in-house employees are particularly sensitive to the degree of commitment demonstrated by senior personnel from a local firm's overseas headquarters. Their understanding of and support for the Japanese subsidiary or branch should be made obvious to reassure everyone involved on the Japanese side that the company is in Japan for the long-term. This has implications for the required status of the firm in Japan, making a Japanese-registered company far more attractive as a more permanent presence to prospective buyers. Along with this there are issues of corporate image and local product image which also need careful development to portray stability, security and commitment.

Head office commitment in some firms was illustrated by how often senior managers visited the subsidiary, beyond what was required for 'crisis' management. Also, what kinds of training programmes, staff exchanges and market research exercises were carried out. How proactive managers were towards building and expanding their presence there, rather than treating it as a secondary market for surplus output.

In terms of power-sharing and decision-making the rank of the main UK representative for Japan and the comparable rank of the subsidiary's senior manager in the company's overall hierarchy are key indicators of commitment. These are even more significant if these positions are held by Japanese managers. Good managers in Japan maintained 'political' links with senior managers at home and were given the opportunity to participate in board-level decision-making relevant to the Japanese operation.

Early problems in a number firms were traced back to the use of 'second-class' or inexperienced managers in establishing the initial office in Japan, for example, or failing to decide on a clear strategy and an adequate level of investment in Japan at the most senior level from the outset. These kinds of mistakes had repercussions long after they were rectified, in terms of the 'reputation' effects for the firm and its products in Japan. Furthermore, those responsible for deciding on entry strategy and investment horizons or the minimum 'payback' period for the Japan operation should have the experience of Japan or at least the conviction and belief in experienced company representatives to give them the patience to plan for the long-term.

Learn the language, learn the way of doing business, become part of the informal networks, build up the confidence of your new workforce and demonstrate long term commitment to your local business partners. Show that you are investing for the long term by waiting until prospective customers recognise your products and company name as part existing industrial infrastructure and are confident enough to approach you for what you have to offer.

Senior-level commitment and the broader corporate strategy vis-a-vis Japan both relate directly to a company's long term plans for its Japan operation. Specific plans amongst the sample firms naturally varied according to their existing status and the outlook for their specific markets in Japan. The majority of firms were either in the process of expansion or aimed to expand in the near future, despite the current recession. Only in a few cases would this involve investing in local manufacturing operations. The costs of this have always been high and continue to grow to the point that even Japanese manufacturers are now investing large amounts of capital setting up production units in the cheap labour countries of south-east Asia and China. By far the most firms were diversifying and broadening their range of products and services in response to the growing competitiveness of foreign products and the deterioration of long-standing supplier-buyer relationships amongst Japanese companies.

In many cases expansion would also involve a move into sales, marketing and distribution activities to get closer to customers and either work closer alongside contracted sales teams and distributors or establish independent sales and distribution functions. Again this was to take advantage of new flexibilities or freedom in the local market structures and the growing importance of cost-saving brought about by recessionary pressures. Some firms envisaged a strengthening of joint-ventures and alliances with local Japanese firms, others saw this as a time to break off past agreements and push for independence. Although the independent route represented the optimal path ahead for many SMEs the costs of developing an in-house sales force and bypassing the distribution chain was seen as too expensive for smaller companies and collaborative 'partnerships' with Japanese distributors remained the best option.

Another change either anticipated or in progress as a result of the broader economic upheavals mentioned above was the move towards taking on Japanese clients for companies that had dealt in the past only with other foreign firms in Japan. In one example a company in the construction industry had recently entered into a new and unusual role as a project manager on local sites employing Japanese sub-contractors.

SMEs involved in trading in particular, with long-term experience in Japan and a good knowledge of local markets, are currently discovering new openings for imported products and are pushing overseas manufacturers to get a foot in the market during this period of change. One larger company had recently expanded its own sales and distribution division with the added remit to identify local market openings and match these up with existing overseas suppliers to boost imports.

Most of the SMEs dealing with high-technology products and carrying out a significant amount of product development locally, usually as sub-contractors to Japanese companies, had plans to increase local facilities for technical support and joint product development with customers. In two cases this simply meant strengthening the subsidiary's engineering division and placing more specialists from UK in Japan. In two other, larger companies this meant relatively large scale investments in separate R&D (predominantly applied product development) facilities outside Tokyo which were already underway.

One of the main messages about commitment from the managers I talked to was to make it 'visible'. The point being that Japanese customers and supporting organisations (suppliers, distributors, retailers, service providers etc..) need to see clearly that the foreign firm is in Japan for the long-term, that they can by relied upon, and that they are building lasting relationships within the local business community. This is done through normal advertising, with a focus on the stability and reliability of the company, rather than on specific products. It is also achieved by promoting the firm at 'socio-business' gatherings, and through membership of specific industry-related organisations. Trade fairs and exhibitions are also useful and there are an estimated 680 in Japan each year to choose from.

Business gatherings are very important in Japan for reinforcing specific networks and groupings. They may be held, for example, to mark the opening of a new local facility, celebrate the appointment of a new company president or to seal a joint-venture agreement. But it is through these that foreign managers can announce their presence and 'present the face' or image of their company. Similarly membership and active involvement in trade associations or industry organisations can fulfil the same objectives and provide the opportunity to learn about the network infrastructures and alliances relevant to one's business. In many cases membership will be Japanese-dominated and it may well not be possible for foreign managers or for particular companies to join.

Most managers suggested that the connections and kudos that can arise from the above kinds of networking activity are more important than legal agreements or on-paper commitments between companies in Japan. This is in keeping with findings in the field of management studies that illustrate a Japanese preference for verbal agreements and informal relationships as the basis for inter-firm alliances. Reputation and credibility are all-important to the success of foreign firms in Japan and commitment to maintaining a long-term presence must be seen to underpin these.

Before moving on to look at how government agencies can help SMEs export to Japan and establish a base in the Japanese market we will focus on a critical factor for successful market entry, that of product or service adaptation.

Customer requirements and the buyer-supplier relationships

Choosing an appropriate entry route into Japan, spending time establishing local contacts, and securing finance for the initial investment are obviously all important start-up activities. But a firm's products and services have to sell locally if the venture is to succeed, and to sell they need to be adapted to meet the requirements of local customers.

Managers responsible for a company's operations in Japan need to understand what Japanese corporate buyers and consumers want from their suppliers and what steps they need to take to fulfil these requirements. The lessons from our SME sample varied a great deal according to the products, services and local activities of the firm in question. So this section will focus in particular on firms who had taken steps to establish technical support and product development operations in Japan, alongside their customers (see Figure 1.1). These are the firms, often in high-technology manufacturing areas, who responded most visibly to the demands of the local market and who provide an illustration for others to aim for.

The general guidelines for foreign companies are very similar, whether they are sub-contracting to Japanese companies, selling to customers direct, or selling via agents or distributors. The quality and reliability of the product sold are of the utmost importance to winning market share. This remains the case despite the fact that recent changes have heightened the relative importance of price as a factor. The credibility of the product brand and the company's overall image are also important to Japanese buyers and underlie the importance of advertising in the consumer markets and specific forms of product promotion in the corporate sector. After-sales service, technical support and the promise of long-term back-up from a supplier or salesman, beyond the one-off purchase is also extremely important in Japan.

Detailed interviews with both British suppliers and Japanese buyers provided insights into the adaptations required and these can be divided into three related areas: (i) product changes, (ii) service and support, and (iii) the buyer-supplier relationship.

Product changes

Product changes tend to be required to suit individual markets wherever they may be, but there are additional requirements in Japan that underlie its special difficulties. Key factors are customization, quality, reliability and what we can call 'features', all closely related. What is essential for managers new to Japan to understand is that it is not simply a matter of improving these aspects of their products but more a question of redefining them according to very different Japanese buyers perceptions and requirements.

Customization, again necessary for most markets, involves adapting the standard product to suit the specific requirements of individual customers. In Japan buyers treat this is a basic requirement rather than an added bonus and foreign companies in Japan quickly gain a reputation for being able, or not able, to customise well. In some cases it is a simple matter of taking account of what the customer wants and responding quickly and efficiently to adapt the product accordingly ('reactive' adaptation). A major difference in Japan is the level of changes often insisted upon by the customer. Very detailed changes are often required, which sometimes have no obvious connection with the efficiency of the product in its intended use. But customization in Japan, more than anywhere else means changing the product and everything associated with it to suit what the customer wants, not what the manufacturer thinks the customer wants. The experience of one British exporter from the survey illustrates this.

This example comes from a company selling customised wheels to OEMs in Japan. An early request was made by the company's main Japanese agent and distributor to improve the quality of the casting finish on the *inside* of the wheel where tiny pits and some rough areas could be found in the section which attaches to the car axle. The UK company queried the request as its various models had sold well in US and UK markets without the change. Moreover, the adaptation would require changes at the machining level and thus involve additional costs.

According to the Japanese firm, however, the fact that this was purely a cosmetic flaw and there was only a small chance that the final customer would come across it was superseded by the poor quality image it portrayed. As an imperfection it indicated to Japanese buyers (retailers and garages as well as final customers) that other faults may exist and product sales would suffer as a result of this perception. In response to these complaints, which came relatively early in the company's link with the Japanese distributor, the manufacturer invested to improve the casting process and create a smoother wheel finish. Looking back at this change, which had been unnecessary in their UK and other overseas markets, a senior manager in the UK saw it as a critical step in their firms longer-term success in Japan.

This kind of investment, in response to buyer demands can be costly for an SME. It is also often risky, where market research comes from a distance, customer response is speculative and returns are uncertain. Balancing the extra efforts required in Japan a large number of respondents emphasised the benefits they gained elsewhere from making the changes required to break into its tough markets. Customization of products in the above sense is closely linked to general quality improvements.

A senior manager in one of the industrial instruments manufacturers stated that demand for higher levels of quality in the company's Japanese markets had led to corporate-wide changes in quality control, testing and production. The company had adopted a target for 0.1 percent failure rate in products coming off the line which had forced wholesale changes in design, materials testing and on-line checking activities. These changes had in turn altered the firm's purchasing requirements and pushed sub-contractors and suppliers to improve their quality levels. In the 6 months following the change in policy at the company's UK headquarters the company had achieved a 'turn around', averaging 0.5-0.6 percent failure rates across all its sub-components and realised a range of spin-off improvements to other products and down to suppliers.

Other forms of customization involve a 'proactive' approach to the Japanese market, rather than reacting to changes and improvements demanded by buyers. To begin to sell in Japan, or to expand and diversify from an existing market foothold, for an 'outsider' in particular, requires active anticipation of customer needs.

The most successful examples of this in terms of product adaptation in our survey came from two firms producing different products for different local markets but sharing a proactive customer-led product development strategy.

A British manufacturer of fluids and steam-processing equipment, used in industrial plants and in domestic-use buildings markets and sells in Japan via its wholly-owned branch. Managers in Japan recognised at an early stage that the local market for their components was dominated by smaller end users and uses, stemming from the higher cost of floor space and the more compact buildings in Japan. This placed a premium on lower specification components and on space-saving innovations in various types of equipment. Moreover they understood that 'me-too' products would not sell well given the extensive local track records and technical service advantages held by their main competitors. The key to their eventual success lay in convincing R&D and production divisions in UK to invest in a new model of a standard component that encompassed all these changes and incorporated added features to those marketed by the competition.

Another manufacturer produced precision measuring instruments and, in addition to a wholly-owned subsidiary in Japan to sell its products, it had developed a technical centre to provide local support services and modify products with direct customer-input. In this sector improvements in the accuracy of the measuring instruments confers a competitive advantage on the manufacturing operations of the end-user, so close ties between instrument buyer or user and supplier exist. Changes in the organisation of the buyers' industry direct the product development strategy of the supplier, not only in Japan but globally, as the Japanese buyer is at the forefront in this area of manufacturing.

When the buyer firm decided to streamline its manufacturing operations, by having certain measuring functions carried out by less-skilled on-line personnel rather than using specialist technical staff on the plant floor, the instrument supplier had to make the necessary design changes. Seeing this as a long-term change in demand trends across a wide variety of instruments, the British subsidiary acted, in some cases ahead of customer demands, to make its products more robust, more mobile and easier to use ('one-button operation'). In addition to more user-friendly instructions and manuals (ie. that can be followed by a non-specialist) the 'front-end' graphics which the equipment used were improved so that a newcomer to a particular measuring task could quickly learn how to do it efficiently. This took account of the fact that on-line personnel were frequently rotated around the plant and had to be able to master new tasks quickly to reduce 'down-time'.

Proactive product customization is all part of keeping ahead in any market, but with the levels of competition that exist amongst component suppliers in Japan it is a necessity, especially in high-technology sectors. Incremental innovation within existing product lines is also important, bringing us to the value placed on added product 'features' in Japan. As suggested above 'me-too' products do not sell well in Japan, particularly if they are sold by foreign companies. Final goods consumers look for something that is different and 'better' in addition to the standard quality and reliability requirements. Corporate buyers are interested in how a component or product can help them get ahead of their own competitors. So, where possible, added features should be built into the product and should be extensively advertised as differentiating characteristics.

The companies surveyed that had taken on board these requirements continually identified key features of competitor products and improved on them directly, as part of their product development strategy. Hence the incidence of product or model 'churning' in Japan with endless versions, makes and updates of consumer products being aggressively advertised, marketed and sold. In several cases subsidiaries changed the model names of products from their UK versions to reflect the added features they incorporated. They also made considerable efforts to alter marketing material and product brochures to reflect this demand for added features.

Even for companies that were not adapting actual products a great deal for

Japan, changes to marketing material, instruction manuals and other product-related literature were considered a critical part of the customization process. Customer demand for quality encompasses the 'quality' of promotional material, technical information, and other literature associated with the product, in addition to product quality. Again, it is critical for those actually doing the adapting to understand fully how the target users define quality.

A good example of this was given by an engineering manager in a Japanese company which regularly bought from a British supplier:

> Instructions in general for operating, maintaining or changing plant equipment need to be more extensive, detailed and specific and user-friendly for our needs. For example, where a company's brochure says 'installation must be carried out by a person with appropriate experience and expertise' we would need this to be changed to state specifically what that expertise should be (i.e. stipulate what specialist technical skills the installation engineer must have).

Two respondents amongst the British suppliers had been asked to change their instruction material entirely, specifically to include user-friendly characters (stick figures, or cartoon drawings etc..) to make them easy to use for non-specialist on-line personnel. This is a common and highly effective way of communicating technical information in Japan, used widely in the consumer electronics industry (in video, TV and fax instruction manuals for example), and seems to be associated with the Japanese fondness for *manga* (cartoon) comic books. One of the abovementioned companies went on to adopt some aspects of the revised manual style in other regional markets because it saved considerably on translation costs.

As regards sales material in some cases effort and investment went into general improvements to existing literature in terms of presentation, style and so on, for Japan and this literature was later used by other company divisions in other markets. But more often changes would be made to suit the Japanese buyer specifically, beyond simple translation. Brochures for example were developed to present an image of the overall company and to emphasise its key 'features' such as technical expertise in a specialised area, or local service and support facilities.

Corporate customers in particular look for signs or proof of engineering capability and customer commitment in sales material. If these characteristics are not openly displayed it may be assumed the supplier is weak in these areas. Technical details relating to the company's products are also popular, in keeping with the extra attention paid to accurate specifications and test and performance data by the average Japanese buyer. Several companies had developed individual leaflets for specific product ranges or models with elaborate graphics and colour pictures describing every aspect.

The main point is that Japanese customers often expect a great deal of say in how products should be adapted and, if the link is with a company who is buying in bulk or building a long-term relationship with a supplier, they may want to become more involved in the adaptation process than British firms are used to. To succeed in Japan British managers have to be prepared to adapt this aspect of their management to fit more closely with Japanese expectations of inter-firm relationships. This may well require more sharing of sensitive information which can lead to problems, often because this kind of information represents a competitive advantage in these kinds of industry sectors. Unfortunately there is no watertight guarantee, even with Japanese companies in Japan, that other firms are going to behave 'honourably' once given access to privileged information in the spirit of inter-firm cooperation. Judging who to trust at this level was one of the more difficult challenges for the technology-intensive firms we spoke to.

Service and support

Although, again, this varied across companies there was a general consensus amongst our survey respondents that Japanese buyers have a very different expectations of after-sales service and technical support, to the point that suppliers must redefine what they offer alongside product sales in Japan. For some British firms the big difference is that some aspects of service and support in Japan are expected in many cases as part of product package, ie. not entailing any additional cost for the buyer.

Related to this, we came across different views on warranties or guarantees, offered with products. Some managers offered these as an assurance that the company was prepared to take on the responsibility for after-sales faults and that this demonstrated a confidence in the product to the Japanese buyer. Others suggested that Japanese buyers saw guarantees as an indication that the supplier was not willing to offer after-sales service and support automatically or as 'a sign of respect' or commitment to the buyer, without some legal document stating their responsibility.

Buyer companies in general expect long-term commitment to after-sales service, backing up the product bought. This explains Japanese purchasing departments' interest in the broader attributes of a supplier firm, particularly local service facilities, but also overall technical experience and expertise. If problems do occur with a product after it has been bought Japanese buyers do want prompt service from the supplier, but the timing of the supplier's response is often not the most important criteria on which they are judged. Japanese companies often want detailed information and a clear illustration of the steps being taken by the supplier to rectify the situation and improve the product. This may include for example technical performance data and details of the supplier's long-term R&D programme relating to the product in question. The buyer wants to be reassured of the supplier's continued commitment to that product and its performance and they may not simply accept a replacement without this assurance.

There are a host of ways that British companies have adapted (or not) to these requirements in Japan in order to satisfy existing customers and win new ones. In most of the firms examined selling technical products their Japan office was taken up with after-sales service and support far more than their counterparts in other markets. One obvious need is for technical personnel to be involved directly in the marketing and sales of products, far more than in the UK. One Japanese manager described the 'human' relationship between the customer's engineer and the supplier's engineer as the most critical of all. Successful British sub-contractors in high-technology industries in Japan, for example, invest to develop direct links between production, engineering and R&D departments in the UK and their Japanese customers. They also use Japan-based engineering staff to pitch to potential customers using precise knowledge of their product technologies, to provide expert support to existing customers and to absorb and pass-on local customer requirements to UK managers.

Companies that can afford it establish technical support centres in Japan to enable technical staff work on-site with corporate customers (two of the sample companies had set up such centres in the last few years). Their main use is for the design, development and customization of products alongside the end user. Local engineers carry out some activities independently and others with additional support from the UK. Overall, a technical centre will facilitate communication between UK-based divisions and Japan-based representatives responsible for meeting customer requirements. In addition to repair and back-up services these can be used as a marketing tool to host demonstrations and display a firm's range of engineering capabilities as well as products.

Buyer-supplier relationships

Various comments above indicate the slightly different nature of the buyer-supplier relationship in Japan. Buyers often demand closer technical 'involvement' and a great deal of technical information about the product and about support services offered. Many Japanese companies strongly favour the development of close working relationships between their technical personnel and those in the supplier firm. This partly explains the evolution of traditional long-term inter-company links within *keiretsu* families and other corporate groups in Japan.

Overall, Japanese customers have high expectations. Underlying these expectations there is a different concept of what it is a consumer or corporate customer is actually buying when a transaction is carried out. In Japan, particularly between companies, a purchase is often not seen as a one-off event or a short-term arrangement decided solely by price (although because of current pressures things are moving towards more flexible, price-led markets). A supplier is traditionally seen as entering into a longer-term commitment, ensuring their product will perform as promised as long as the buyer uses it. This commitment involves ensuring reliable delivery and maintaining 'stable' prices, plus technical advice, service and efficient repair and maintenance support. In effect the buyer is purchasing the expertise, resources and experience of the supplier associated with a particular product.

Most Japanese suppliers and manufacturers, which British firms compete against in their Japanese (and perhaps global) markets, have developed this high level of customer commitment in every division and at every level, rather than leaving the responsibility solely to front-line marketing or service staff (although it is less in evidence amongst Japanese firms when they are selling abroad). It is the devolvement of responsibility to every level of the corporation that is said to partly underlie the broader success of Japanese manufacturing firms.

One Japanese manager, with experience of living and working in the UK, put it in these terms:

In Japanese companies the high level of personal responsibility taken on by each employee on behalf of the whole firm means that each will apologise directly for any mistakes or failures relating to their product or service, no matter who was actually responsible. They will also tend to take it upon themselves to rectify the situation, at least by referring it to the appropriate individual or division. This contrasts with employee attitudes in the UK who to separate their personal job responsibilities from those of other employees in their firm. A buyer calling the wrong department of a British supplier is likely to receive very little assistance. Individuals will not make it their responsibility unless they have an allocated role to assist buyers. In Japan, no matter what position or remit a manager or employee has, first and foremost they represent the entire firm in dealings with customers (in fact with anyone outside the firm).

This philosophy is associated with the more famous aspects of manufacturing management in Japanese firms. '*Kaizen*' or 'continuous improvement' is better translated as: 'an *enthusiasm* for improvement at every level of employee'. Similarly, this work place attitude derives from the strong social obligations that are a characteristic of Japanese society, some of them unusual to an outsider. An example of this, suggested by a Japanese manager, describes the case of a car accident in Japan where guilty party is expected to apologise directly to the aggrieved party. This is not a legal requirement but there is a strong enough social obligation in Japan that the police will ensure that an appropriate apology has been made.

Taking this to its extreme some would say that the overall reputation of a firm and its credibility as a respectable company is at stake with each individual transaction. The point is that if this is believed by all employees in a supplier company and each takes personal responsibility to ensure everything is done to fulfil this commitment then the company will be truly customer-led. This provides some insight into the market 'environment' in which Japanese manufacturers have evolved and therefore an indication of how British suppliers must adapt.

Government support at both ends

To complete this chapter on foreign firms' initial entry into Japan we will look at some sources of advice and support for British companies in the early stages of exploration and investment. Various sources of information exist to help foreign companies plan and implement their entry strategy into Japan. The most common cited in a 1994 survey by JETRO include (in order of frequency): research companies and consultancy firms; lawyers and law offices; accountants and auditors; office of Japanese sales agent in home country; branch of Japanese trading company in home country; branch of Japanese financial institution in home country, and; publications regarding Japan. All of which were used extensively by the British SMEs included in this survey.

Beyond these sources, firms that are interested in selling to Japan or establishing an office in Japan, particularly small firms without the financial resources to go it alone, will often look to public sector agencies and government support schemes for advice or assistance in the early stages of their approach. The following sections examine some of the support mechanisms on offer from the British Government and compare these with schemes in operation from other countries. We also take a look at the policies of various Japanese agencies to encourage foreign firms to do business with and in Japan, which have evolved as a response to the burgeoning trade deficit described earlier in this book. A number of useful addresses are listed in the Appendix at the end of this book, as starting points for British companies interesting in the Japanese market.

Because government assistance to, and intervention in, the private sector is essentially a political issue, subject to the 'public relations' mentality of government officials, this section will take the experience and views of company managers as its starting point to review what is being done to help British SMEs enter the Japanese market. It will then provide more recent information about government support that SMEs looking to Japan should be aware of.

Help from the British government

When asked about British government schemes and assistance mechanisms most of the sample SMEs spoke about the British Embassy in Japan and the various DTI initiatives designed to help firms set up in Japan or export to Japan. Most managers had heard of, or experienced at first hand, the various efforts of these bodies and were unanimous in their belief that UK government offices were the best initial starting point for any firms considering their first steps into the Japanese market.

However, there was a mixed reaction as to the perceived effectiveness of some public-sector efforts and a wide range of opinions as to possible improvements. Managers also tended to compare and contrast these efforts with private sector initiatives, such as the British Chamber of Commerce in Japan (BCCJ) and the British Market Council, and with assistance mechanisms set up by other national agencies, particularly the American Embassy, the American Chamber of Commerce in Japan (ACCJ), the EC-Japan Centre and the European Business Council (EBC) as well as the range of Japanese initiatives to encourage foreign trade and investment (see below).

Support received The sample companies can be divided into three groups in terms of the level of support received from British government sources: those with direct experience of specific assistance schemes (7/30); those that interact with agency staff on regular basis and keep in touch with Japan-related initiatives when they appear, but have not participated in schemes (14/30), and; those that have little or no contact and no knowledge of such initiatives (9/30).

7 companies out of the 30 full case studies had actually commissioned DTI or Embassy services at some time or other, that is, paid money to obtain services or participated in a subsidised visit. The most common services used were the market research services, either commissioned in the London or at the Embassy in Tokyo. Relatively few companies had participated in trade missions (two of the managers interviewed had come to Japan initially as part of a mission) although many managers had come to Japan before such schemes had been established. In more recent years it is likely that level of participation has grown. The number of missions increased to 123 in 1992-3 and involved 2,350 participants, with the stated aim for missions to contain 60 percent of participants from SMEs.

There was a great deal of direct experience amongst interviewees of the now-famous Executive Training Programme (ETP) organised through the EC-Japan Centre and sponsored by the EU, which has been going for many years and built up a formidable reputation as a way for new managers to gain useful insights into doing business in Japan. OSTEMS missions were considered less relevant for most of the SMEs but the Engineers to Japan Scheme had been used by several firms and was praised, particularly as a way for firms to gain quick but useful insights into Japanese manufacturing methods and new technologies.

The majority of firms (21/30, including the 7 above) that kept in touch with government agencies and kept abreast of new initiatives most valued the information exchange and 'networking' roles offered by the DTI and the Embassy. They could also provide a valuable service checking the credibility or reputation of Japanese companies as preparation for a joint-venture or a buyer-supplier arrangement. For new firms both were said to be a good source of market information and expert contacts, 'good starting points for new entrants'.

Others had received help with product exhibition and export promotion activities. There was also specific praise for the Market Entry Guarantee Scheme (MEGS, now ended) and other loans systems which helped SMEs to research and test their market in Japan without fully committing investment finance. '*Japan News*', the newsletter of the Action Japan Campaign, from the 'Exports to Japan Unit of the DTI, had been used by some and was described as a very useful round-up of relevant news and advice for newcomers to Japan.

For SMEs that had been in Japan for some time the Embassy still acted as a useful contact point for negotiating with Japanese government officials and providing high-profile backing for commercial bids and semi-political leverage for companies trying to get into restricted markets.

Of a range of specialist information services useful for experienced managers particular praise from two firms was for a series of quarterly construction industry bulletins providing information on forthcoming large-scale international projects that Japanese contractors were bidding for, written by the Embassy's commercial section. A couple of other firms also mentioned Embassy and DTI support helping companies entering into third country projects with Japanese partners.

The remaining 9 companies that had little knowledge of government schemes and little contact with DTI or Embassy staff are predominantly subsidiaries managed by Japanese representatives who either saw little of use in the services offered or had no knowledge of the functions of the relevant agencies. It is significant (although unsurprising) that it was mainly Japanese respondents who had the least amount of contact with British government initiatives. In many cases amongst these firms there was a belief that the general role of the Embassy was a political one rather than to provide private sector assistance.

Problems with services and suggested improvements Amongst any group of
managers there are always those that are overly-critical of government support
initiatives, either because they have a strict 'free market' ethos, or because they
have problems with the mechanisms or public-sector organisations that provide
this support. Most of the interviewees in this survey saw definite benefits for
SMEs in Japan resulting from the provision of government assistance, but also
identified problems and possible improvements to the services they had experienced or observed. As described later, new measures have been introduced by the
organisations responsible that meet many of these criticisms. Nevertheless, it is
worth mentioning them in order to provide an input into ongoing policy formu-
lation.

Limiting ourselves to the 21 managers that either had direct experience of
British government services or kept in touch with the relevant organisations, one
problem expressed by about a third of them (particularly the smallest, locally-
registered firms) was the lack of official recognition given to YK and KK-
registered independent SMEs in Japan. Companies with head offices in the UK are
entitled to assistance either through the DTI and other offices in London or through
the Embassy in Tokyo (and representatives in Osaka). Companies that are
independently established in Japan are legally Japanese and strictly speaking are
not entitled to government help, although in practice there is some flexibility.
Cutting off these firms would mean ignoring a wealth of management experience
in Japan and a substantial number of SMEs that are responsible for FDI flows and
imports into Japan from the UK. In fact this is acknowledged by government
representatives and partly rectified by their informal contact and assistance to
these firms via, for example, the SAMBI (Small and Medium-Sized Business
Initiative) group (until recently this sub-group of the BCCJ supported SMEs in
Japan).

Other problems with government services cited by managers were as follows
(the number of managers making this criticism appears in brackets):

-      in some sectors, a lack of actual management or market expertise, or
       specialised technology or industry sector experience amongst service
       providers (8/21);

-      a general focus on large firms and higher profile projects at the expense of
       SMEs and sometimes a lack of policy implementation or 'follow-through'
       (7/21);

-      too few resources to assist with detailed local business regulations, such as securing bank loans, getting visas, understanding labour laws, complying with company registration rules, and so on ('a centralised advice centre would be most beneficial for new SMEs') (5/21);

- on occasion, poor interaction and coordination between various agencies and a problem of overlapping remits between UK agencies themselves and with other EC-level groups (in terms of both the provision of support services in Japan and trade-related lobbying from home) (5/21).

These problem areas immediately point to improvements that these SME managers would like to see in British government services. Respondents made a number of additional suggestions about new initiatives that would benefit UK SMEs in Japan, both existing and newcomers. One common idea was for the establishment of a 'one-stop-shop' in Tokyo to serve as a coordinating centre for British services (both private and public), as a comprehensive advice centre, to provide subsidised accommodation for newcomers and as an exhibition area for British products (a more ambitious suggestion was to add shopping and restaurant facilities, all with a distinctly British theme, to help finance the centre). This would build on the MIPRO idea (the Manufacturing Import Promotion Organisation based at Ikebukuro).

A related idea put forward by two different managers was that the British government should sponsor advertisements and public relations exercises in Japan to raise the profile of British products in general amongst consumers. Active marketing of specific products and a good company image plays a central role for both Japanese and foreign companies in Japan and a national campaign could greatly benefit individual company efforts. This is particularly so for SMEs that cannot afford extensive PR exercises. Special emphasis should be placed on the technical sophistication, reliability and quality of British products it was suggested.

Finally there was a more general call for the government to sponsor more visits, of British SME managers to Japan and of Japanese delegations to the UK. These suggestions came with general praise for the existing schemes to subsidise visits and interaction. The expense of visiting Japan to research potential markets and Japanese partners in the initial stages of establishing a presence was said to be a key constraint for British SMEs. Similarly, it would be easier for Japanese trading companies and distributors to come to UK with British government support (not necessarily financial), either as potential partners wishing to assess the capabilities of their British counterpart, or as Japanese firms looking for potential British products to add to their own portfolios. Such support again promotes FDI and trade.

The obvious difficulty with the above suggestions is the lack of resources available to British government agencies to assist the private sector in these areas. However, some of the above criticisms and recommendations suggest ways in which existing schemes could be made more appropriate to the needs of SMEs.

More recent British government support It should be stressed that there was praise for many of the UK government services from the managers that had used them, particularly from more recent entrants who had experienced the newer schemes under the 'Action Japan Campaign', established under Michael Heseltine (then President of the UK government's Board of Trade) in 1994. It must be noted that many of the companies interviewed for this study entered Japan some time ago and many of their experiences of government assistance schemes are dated.

Since 1988 with the setting up of the Japan Trade Group, now called the Action Japan Committee, the British Embassy and the DTI have greatly improved their support services both for large firms and for SMEs. These changes counter many of the criticisms of government services made above.

The Japan Trade Group, comprised of the Chairmen and Chief Executives of around 25 large (and one medium-sized) companies, advises the work of the UK-based support teams (focused at the DTI's Exports to Japan Unit) and the British Embassy's commercial operations in Tokyo and Osaka. It is supported by the smaller, more hands-on Trade Advisory Group which encompasses a wide range of expertise and experience in doing business with Japan. Both are incorporated in the Action Japan initiative, which has a stated aim to increase visible exports to Japan from £2.6 billion in 1993 to £3.5 billion in 1996 (this and much of the following information comes from in-house documents provided by the Exports to Japan Unit, DTI, the Commercial Section of the British Embassy in Tokyo, and various issues of 'Japan News', the DTI newsletter of the Action Japan Campaign).

A major improvement since 1988, for example, is the 9 export promoters, seconded from industry, to work over the last two years with the Exports to Japan Unit to bring their sector-specific experience to bear on DTI support services. To add to this, in 1995 11 priority sectors were selected to further focus export promotion activities. These are: healthcare, automotive components, marine equipment, power generation equipment, construction, speciality chemicals, electronic components, environmental equipment and services, clothing, textile and retailing ('lifestyle'), food and drink, and one called 'major projects worldwide' (in manufacturing and infrastructure). Sector-specific trade promotion plans incorporate trade missions, trade shows, seminars, company visits and a range of information-gathering exercises, all of which support the chargeable services to managers (DTI, 1995a).

The British Embassy's Commercial Department in Japan coordinates and provides these government services in Japan, alongside the Embassy's Science and Technology division and its other diplomatic functions. It also liaises extensively with JETRO (see next section) and other Japanese government organisations, the British Chamber of Commerce in Japan (BCCJ), the British Market Council (a Japanese-funded organisation involved in research, collaborative work and exchanges) and MIPRO. It is assisted by the Information Section of the Embassy, which fulfills a public relations role and acts as a public information office. The Economic Section and the Science and Technology Section also provide support while having their own distinctive roles.

With 8 UK-based staff and 26 locally engaged staff in Tokyo, the British Embassy's Commercial Department is divided into three sections, two dealing with industrial goods and one with consumer goods. It was involved in the following activities in 1994 (listed in British Embassy in-house reports):

- Chargeable services: 204 cases (Jan-Dec 1994)
- Missions: 16 (277 companies to end of November 1994)
- Trade shows: 48 visited, including 13 DTI-supported groups
- Business visitors: 1,081 British, 1,576 local (Jan-Nov 1994)
- Seminars, store
  promotions and
  company events: 23 (167 companies)

Beyond these services the DTI and the Embassy are continually involved in new endeavours to introduce British firms to the market opportunities in Japan and help them overcome some of the initial hurdles. The Commercial Section expects a further increase in British company visits to Japan, with an anticipated total of 31 trade missions and 20 trade fair delegations in 1996/97. Most recently, steps have also been taken to establish working groups with key Japanese companies based in London (the 'London Task Force') to provide an insiders view of export opportunities to Japan and share relevant industry contacts.

At the time of writing there is also discussion of a proposed 'British Industrial Centre' in Japan. This would provide a central facility to accommodate new British entrants, allowing them to share resources and exhibition space and exploit economies of scale through cooperation. Although it would be run on a commercial basis, with tenants paying rent and a fee for facilities, such a centre could potentially fill the need (described above) for a 'one-stop-shop' expressed by managers in our survey (DTI, 1995b).

In general managers we talked to who had used the services of the Exports to Japan Unit (EJU) at the DTI rated it as a good service, including many of the 'pay-as-you-use' schemes. The latter include the Market Information Enquiry

Services, the Export Marketing Research Scheme, the Export Representative Service and the Overseas Status Report Service all organised under the Overseas Trade Services (OTS) run by the DTI and the Foreign and Commonwealth Office and regional agencies such as Scottish Trade International (with 2,000 staff, 13 UK offices and the DTI headoffices in London).

It should still be emphasised that British government schemes are designed to be visible to potential exporters and investors in the UK. They focus on introducing newcomers to potential business opportunities in Japan and therefore tend to have less relevance for firms that have overcome the initial hurdles and are coping with the longer-term problems of managing in Japan. However, for SMEs with limited financial and human resources, it would be a mistake to attempt to begin the process of exporting to Japan or investing in Japan without first exploring what UK government agencies have to offer in the way of assistance.

What are other governments doing to help SMEs in Japan?

Interviewees liked to make comparisons between British government services and those provided by other countries for their firms in Japan. In general several of the larger countries were said to have better-resourced agencies working in or on Japan and some were said to have achieved a closer integration between their private and public sector interests. Managers talked primarily about the various combinations of chambers of commerce, regional development organisations, specialist industry sector groups and the Embassies.

The USA does the most trade with Japan and has the largest number of firms in Japan (42 percent of all FDI in Japan since 1950 is from the USA, compared to 5 percent from the UK) so it follows that US government has substantially more resources to devote to assisting its companies. This is reflected by the range of specialist services on offer from the American Embassy and the influence of its direct lobbying operations in Tokyo and from Washington. However, the American Chamber of Commerce in Japan (ACCJ) was heavily criticised compared to the BCCJ, despite its permanent exhibition of American products being praised by one manager.

The Swedish Embassy was also mentioned by a number of respondents, particularly as a good example of the one-stop-shop idea in practice. Compared to the British the Swedes were noted for concentrating a wide range of relevant commercial services, including a showcase of products, at a single location in Roppongi.

The Australian's were praised for the effectiveness of AUSTRADE and the initiative shown in the 'Market Entry Competition' organised with the government of New Zealand. This scheme to invites businesses and individuals to suggest ways for smaller businesses to introduce products and establish a presence in the Japanese market.

Both the German and the French agencies in Japan were said to be better resourced than the British, and several managers suggested that they had been able to develop industry sector specialists more effectively than is possible in the British system and therefore provide more than an 'introduction' service for new firms.

A specific regional agency representing the region of Brittany was given as an example by one manager of a useful, well-resourced and focused support initiative. The MIRCEB organisation acting as the Chamber of Commerce in Japan for Brittany is oriented towards SMEs with a focus on agricultural products, the main export from the region. It engages in a range of activities including government lobbying for access to specific markets (in a notable success it had recently gained access to Japan's protected pork market), market research for product and sector groups in France and searches for Japanese partners, trading houses and distributors for Brittany-based companies. Similar to the British Embassy MIRCEB charges a commission for some of its specialist activities. The group had also recently become active in France finding appropriate products in Brittany and assessing possible markets in Japan, using existing links with buyers in Japan.

Finally we must include a mention of the European Commission (EC, CEC or EU) activities promoting investment in and trade with Japan. As is characteristic of the CEC a range of DG's (Directorate Generals) have organised a confusing array of initiatives relevant to Japan. As in the case of many past British government initiatives, the CEC's approach has been criticised for its lack of hands-on practicality and the lack of attention to SMEs. But, again similarly, in recent years there have been a range of improvements in these support programmes.

A number of relevant and widely known schemes are coordinated by the EU-Japan Centre for Industrial Cooperation, based in Tokyo. This organisation was established in 1987, with a staff of around 20, and is supported by DGIII (the DG for Industry) and the Ministry for Trade and Industry (MITI) in Japan (Trevor, 1995). Although it is a useful focus for a range of information sources for new businesses in Japan it mainly subsidises and hosts a range of management training programmes that introduce managers and engineers to Japan and to Japanese business practices. These programmes, like the regular Human Resources Training Programmes (HRTP), and missions that focus on specific subjects, such as 'Innovation and Product Development in Japan' (June-July, 1995), include seminars, lectures and visits to companies and research organisations in Japan.

The chance to interact with senior Japanese managers is cited as one of the major benefits of the schemes. There are additional subsidies available for SME representatives from DGXXIII, although much of the subject matter from the training courses has been criticised as being more appropriate for representatives from larger firms.

Other organisations like the European Business Council, the Industrial Cooperation Centre, and other schemes, such as the famous ETP mentioned above, the Industrial Cooperation Programme and the recent 'Gateway to Japan' (1994-96) initiative are all higher profile, wider-ranging schemes than the Commission has run in the past and appear, so far, to be proving more effective in their aims. Gateway to Japan, with an 8 million ECU budget for 1994 (5.3 million is ETP), follows 'Export to Japan' (1990-93) as part of the EXPROM series of initiatives from DGI/F. It focuses mainly on seminars, trade missions and trade fairs and provides some useful (though limited) funding, particularly for SME managers to attend such events. It is certainly worth new entrants investigating these schemes as a first point of call, for financial assistance, information or advice, or as a direct route into the Japan-related business networks covering Europe (CEC, 1995, and CEC DGI Briefing Notes, 1995).

Help from other organisations

In addition to the initiatives discussed above there are a range of organisations and activities that are the result of public-private sector partnerships or lie outside the government-run efforts to assist trade and investment in Japan.

The British Chamber of Commerce in Japan, with almost 300 members, has a considerable influence and acts as a business forum for a range of issues relating to British companies in Japan. It has recently been restructured and has three main Committees, governed by a fourth, top-level Executive Committee. The Programme Planning Committee, a strategic 'think-tank', has replaced what was known as the Trade and Industry (T&I) group. One of its best known sub-groups, the Science and Technology Action Group (STAG), is now a sub-group of the Science and Technology Committee (SciTech). Finally, the Small and Medium-Sized Business Initiative (SAMBI), which was very active at the time of our survey no longer exists and its members interests are covered by the SME Committee.

These fulfil a number of roles for their respective memberships, as a focal point for talks, seminars, advice services and general interaction and for discussing and voicing the concerns of their particular sub-sectors. All have formal links with the relevant commercial and scientific divisions of the British Embassy in Japan, and, through the British Chamber of Commerce network in the UK, to relevant industry associations back home. Each also has a specific range of network contacts to relevant associations and government agencies in Japan. The BCCJ also produces a journal, 'Insight', every two months covering issues of interest to British firms in Japan and those interested in moving into Japan, which published early findings from the survey covered in this book (Collinson, 1994).

STAG, with a membership of over 60 scientists, has grown rapidly since its initiation in 1984 and holds meetings for visiting foreign engineers and scientists in Japan as well as for the established European 'technical fraternity' in Japan. It has produced some excellent texts (like the well-known "*Gaijin* Scientist", *gaijin* meaning foreigner) introducing newcomers to Japan's science and technology environment.

One of the most relevant organisations for UK SMEs was SAMBI. It was established in 1990, had around 40 registered corporate members in Japan, and claimed over 300 man-years of experience in Japan. Its membership was industry wide and it focused explicitly on opportunities to earn revenues for member's businesses. SAMBI held a regular set of talks and discussions each year that related to the particular needs of small businesses in Japan, such as recruitment, banking, finance and taxation, and import-export regulations. At a more informal level it represented an approachable group of extremely experienced British managers in Japan, who continue to meet regularly. Its members all run successful companies locally which are themselves a good source of products and services for new start-ups (from printing and translation services to computing needs and consultancy).

The BCCJ and its sub-groups continue to be important as sources of factual information on regulations and laws affecting foreign businesses in Japan, or business opportunities like exhibitions or special investment loans. But a great deal of this kind of information can also be picked up elsewhere (at the JETRO library in the Kyodo News building near Toranomon station, for instance). What the newcomer cannot get elsewhere is the more 'tacit' knowledge needed to understand how Japan is different from other markets and what steps need to be taken to adapt personally and organisationally to its business environment. The BCCJ members are perhaps the best source of this kind of information for new British businesses.

Other business organisations, based both in Japan and in the UK are worth a brief mention. In addition to the general business organisations, like the Confederation of British Industry (CBI), the Institute of Directors (IOD), and the UK-based Chambers of Commerce (of which London, Bristol and Birmingham have strong Japan links), there are a range of specialist Japan-related groups organised by the private sector. These include the Anglo-Japanese High Technology Forum and the Anglo-Japanese Industrialists Forum (AJIF), both of which bring together representatives from British and Japanese companies for seminars and discussions relating to business between the two countries. The latter is newer but shows signs of being more relevant for smaller firms. But the former has a good, long-standing reputation for attracting very senior people from high-tech companies with interests in Japan.

Alternatively, there are a range of organisations that specialise in export services or advice, like the London-based Institute of Export and various regional export clubs (Scottish Trade International fulfils some of these roles in Scotland). There are also a variety of small business organisations, from the Federation of Independent Businesses to SME divisions of regional chambers of commerce. These are generally excellent starting points for managers looking for sources of help and advice and can often open the way into useful contact networks providing access to colleagues with experience in Japan.

Help from the Japanese government

Amongst the sample firms there was less knowledge about the initiatives on offer from Japanese government agencies to help foreign companies, despite the profusion of schemes being organised. This was partly because the most prominent of these schemes have been targeted explicitly at newcomers and would-be investors abroad, rather than existing firms. There was also some cynicism about the real intentions of Japanese policy makers responsible for recent initiatives (a number of whom were interviewed as part of this project) and about the real effects at the 'ground level' for foreign firms. Criticism of this nature came from both Japanese and British managers and a great deal of uncertainty remains, even within the Japanese government about the direction in which the country is headed vis-a-vis foreign investors and the 'new' approach towards foreign firms in Japan. To some extent public-sector attempts at redressing the trade imbalance and appeasing foreign trading partners (especially the Americans) have been overtaken by economic events over recent years. Imports have grown rapidly and initially only the appreciation of the Yen and the US Dollar's dive in value propped up the imbalance in value terms. Now the structural shift towards more imports, prompted by changing consumption and corporate purchasing patterns, is obvious.

A broad range of organisations in Japan have adapted their remits to encourage inward FDI and imports from overseas, in response to the international pressure on Japan to open its domestic markets. Figure (3.1) provides an overview of some of the key steps taken by the Japanese authorities. Rather than go into detail about the regulatory changes that have been made and the initiatives that have been established this section will focus on British SME experience of these changes.

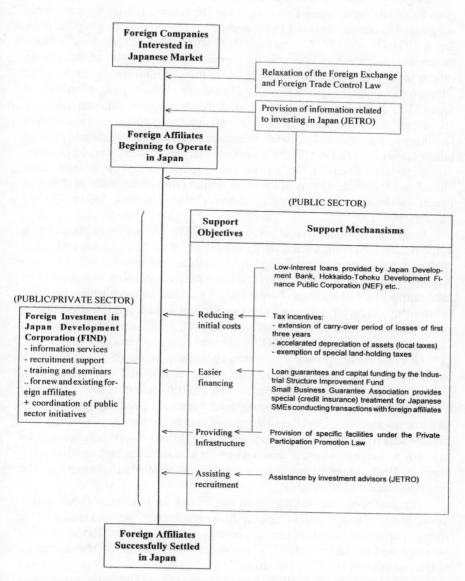

Figure 3.1   Japanese government measures for promoting FDI in Japan

Source: Adapted from JETRO 1994b

Services for new entrants The most prominent of the above-mentioned organisations is JETRO (the Japan External Trade Organisation) which, as its name suggests, was previously (until 1984) engaged in the promotion of exports from Japan. JETRO's staff of 1,200 and budget of 480 million Yen provides assistance to foreign companies in Japan via 50 regional offices and abroad through its offices in 58 countries. This is mainly in the form of information services and advice on all matters relating to exports to Japan and establishing a business in Japan. The organisation has a range of 'investment promotion advisers' (12 abroad) and 'senior trade advisors' (34 abroad), maintains a database for new plant location opportunities and regional investment incentives and a database on local business partners (JETRO 'TOPS'), organises buyers missions abroad (25 each year), sponsors visits for foreign managers, journalists and politicians from abroad and coordinates many of the other similar programmes running under its parent the Ministry of Trade and Industry (MITI) (JETRO, 1993a; JETRO London, 1995).

One of the best-known initiatives from JETRO, established in March 1993, is the Business Support Centre set up in central Tokyo between Roppongi and Kasumigaseki, to provide subsidised office facilities and advice services for new foreign firms in Japan. Just over a year after its start an estimated 50 percent of its total number of 110 users, had apparently succeeded in 'establishing business relationships in Japan'. Of the 67 firms detailed on its past and future occupants list at this time, 6 were British firms compared to 18 Americans, three French, one German and 5 Portuguese (JETRO, 1993b, and interview data).

One case study firm was deliberately chosen as a former BSC occupant with experience of some of the other recent initiatives set up by JETRO. This firm and most others that had come into contact with the BSC saw it as one of the most useful of the new assistance mechanisms, with very good facilities to help newcomers and also providing a degree of credibility for firms entering into negotiations with local Japanese companies for the first time. Although it may be too early to judge two central drawbacks were said to be the lack of advertising about the BSC and the relatively limited number of resident offices that could be accommodated.

Another prominent initiative run by JETRO are the Study Programmes, 'Invest in Japan' and 'Export to Japan', which organise seminars and field trips for foreign participants on short-term introductory visits to Japan. The latter is the oldest of the two and has helped 68 British participants in its 19 programmes up to the end of 1994 (JETRO, 1994b).

An initiative alongside JETRO, which began in June 1993 when pressure on the Japanese government to assist new foreign companies in Japan was at its most intense, is the Foreign Investment in Japan Development Corporation ('FIND'). FIND is a private company established with a great deal of Japanese government support to provide consulting, contract research, training, information and support services to overseas companies exploring opportunities in Japan. It has developed into a good source of information on market opportunities as well as on the on-going changes in government regulations and incentives pertaining to foreign firms in Japan (FIND, 1994; FIND, 1993, and promotional literature).

The three sample SMEs that had established themselves in Japan very recently had reasonably good knowledge of the Japanese government agencies and the assistance they had to offer. Although, the manager setting up a local subsidiary for a financial services company had discounted the validity of most government help given his company's activities (most schemes are targeted at importers and local investors). This had led him to overlook some useful information and advisory publications on-hand at the BSC and at JETRO's main library which could have provided help on the practicalities of renting office space, registering the company locally, understanding the local taxation system and so on. The other two newcomers knew a great deal about what was on offer, had used most of the advice services available and found most of the other schemes more appropriate for later stages of activity.

There was something of a contrast between these three firms and the rest of sample. Most managers who had been in Japan for some time no longer kept in touch with these government agencies or monitored the changes in assistance to foreign firms. In many cases it was thought that assistance was only on offer for new entrants and while managers may have used JETRO's information services during their initial period in Japan they did not believe it had anything to offer them now. In some cases it was evident that firms were overlooking subsidised information services and sources of specialist sector advice on offer from JETRO while carrying out their own research or contracting private consultants to investigate markets for them.

Loans schemes and tax incentives The government services that are of relevance to existing foreign SMEs tend to be promoted through JETRO but operated from other organisations, most under the MITI 'umbrella'. The Japan Development Bank (JDB) has greatly expanded its various schemes to provide loans to foreign affiliated companies since 1984, particularly with the start of two programmes: 'Facilities for Imported Products' and 'Promotion of Foreign Direct Investment in Japan'. The JDB has over 100 different loan programmes, mainly for companies making capital investments and R&D expenditures, where it will provide 30-50 percent of total funds with the maximum interest rate set at the standard bank rate and the average loan term is 15 years. The Export-Import Bank of Japan (JEXIM) also has a programme to assist non-Japanese firms exporting manufactured goods to Japan (JETRO, 1994b).

There was a generally poor take up of these new loans schemes amongst the smaller sample companies we looked at, for two apparent reasons. Poor advertising and promotion at the management level, contrasting the loud noises made at the political level, is the first. Most managers did not know of the existence of most schemes or, again, thought they were only available for new entrants. Those that did use loans tended to have heard about them through informal contacts. A more significant reason was the specifications and guarantees needed before companies qualified for assistance plus the various constraints placed on the use of loans. In many cases, for example, finance is only available for local investments in manufacturing facilities, which smaller SMEs are not involved in.

Five companies from the sample had, at some time or another, received loan assistance through a government agency. The only small firm was KK-registered enabling it to qualify for low-interest funds from the Small and Medium Sized Business Federation. The others were all large SMEs, including the company that received a £850,000 loan from the Japan Development Bank, through the Bank of Tokyo, which was part of MITI's 'Structural Improvement Fund' (described earlier). Another used a factory owned in the USA (visited by the Japanese officials involved) as a capital guarantee for a low interest loan from the JDB and a second received a loan for the development of a local manufacturing facility.

A wider range of SMEs had experienced tax-related and tariff-related benefits indirectly from government assistance schemes. Again, most of these came from MITI via for example its International Trade Administration Bureau (Import Division) for tax relief on imports, its International Business Affairs Division (Industrial Policy Bureau) for tax incentives under the new investment law to facilitate recovery of investment costs for new businesses (only for firms established in the past 5 years), or even its Export-Import Insurance Division. But most managers suggested their companies had benefited 'by default' from these schemes, the incentives being on the whole too small to warrant significant changes in their own investment or importing practices. One manager that had gone out of his way to qualify for an Import Promotion Scheme from the Ministry of Finance in 1989, providing tax aid and various incentives for importers, had found a significant number of 'hidden' conditions attached to the benefits significantly reducing the reward for his efforts.

Overall it is difficult to judge how effective these schemes are in helping foreign SMEs in Japan. None of the sample firms had entered Japan as a result of JETROs overseas trade advisory activities, for example, but many of these mechanisms had been established after the majority of them had come to Japan, when there were few special schemes available. Newcomers had benefited to a certain extent but until recently it appears that only a small proportion of new entrants used the services on offer. Discussions with MITI officials as part of this survey revealed that they do very little research into what the local effects of these initiatives are, in terms of how many firms benefit, or whether they even counteract the acknowledged barriers that still exist.

There is certainly a lack of knowledge amongst experienced SME managers about what assistance is available and in some cases this is tied to a general feeling that Japanese government agencies still primarily restrict foreign firms rather than help them. One Japanese manager suggested many of JETRO's schemes were in fact 'window dressing' to fulfil a political role and made little impact at ground level. Largely because of this attitude managers had few suggestions as to how local agencies could further assist them, beyond addressing the range of impediments listed earlier.

Having said this it is certainly the case that initiatives established by JETRO and other government agencies have greatly improved over the past few years, in terms of their effectiveness in helping foreign companies move into Japan, and in the growing range of companies coming into contact with and benefiting from these services.

To sum up, all of the managers and consultants involved in this study advised newcomers to Japan to make sure they gained what information and support they could from the British, Japanese and other agencies, rather than entirely 'going it alone'. General information and market data covering specific sectors, contacts and introductions, strategic advice on how to approach and deal with Japanese business people and government agencies, and so on, is all available to a certain degree from various sources and these should not be ignored as good basic starting points.

When it comes to government support, from any source, most managers involved in entering a new market and setting up new branch for their business will want to get as much as they can in the way of free information, advertising, loans and so on from the public-sector and, in many cases, they want to do as little as possible to get it. As a consequence most will tend to complain that insufficient support or inadequate funding is given to their companies (especially small firms), but at the same time acknowledge that it is a competitive world and ultimately success or failure is down to themselves and their product or service.

It was generally felt by managers and many government officials alike, however, that improvements could be made in the overall structure for the provision of support services for foreign firms in Japan. This could include a strengthening of links between the British and the Japanese agencies involved in offering very similar services to provide joint support and promote a more coordinated effort.

To end this section on a political note, there was also some demand from both Japanese and British interviewees for a clearer division of responsibilities between national and European-level agencies, especially to make Japanese government lobbying more effective. It was thought that a united EC-front (partly attempted by organisations like the EBC and the EC-Japan Centre), even a European Chamber of Commerce, would present a stronger commercial and political organisation to match the Americans.

Overall, this chapter has described the process and the problems of the initial market entry and start-up of SME operations in Japan. The basic lessons from our study suggest that firms looking to export to Japan or establish a base in Japan should consult the government agencies providing information, advice and support, both in the UK and in Japan, as an essential first step. Beyond this the actual mode of entry and the selection of initial business partners in Japan are critical factors affecting the long-term success or failure of the enterprise, requiring investment into research and preparation before a specific path is chosen. Understanding the relevant business networks, locating and using experienced local advisors and adapting products, services and the management approach to suit 'local conditions' from day-one are all essential. All of which requires UK-based SMEs to place their best managers in charge of the endeavour and to show patience and a deep commitment to long-term business relationships in Japan.

Chapter 4 now looks at some of the longer-term problems and benefits of managing a business in Japan.

4 Managing in Japan

A major aim of this study was to gain an insight into the main difficulties facing British SMEs in Japan, and into the ways successful firms had overcome these. In this chapter we will examine some of the major constraints of operating in Japan, compared to other overseas markets, then look specifically at some of the *management* problems companies experienced with their operations in Japan. The focus in the latter section will be on the difficulties of integrating the very different Western and Japanese management cultures, attracting, keeping and organising good local staff, setting and implementing strategy from a distance (in the case of SMEs with UK headquarters) and interacting with Japanese companies as customers, suppliers and competitors on a regular basis. Finally, the last section will look at how British companies can learn from their Japanese counterparts and derive some of the benefits of being in one the toughest markets alongside some of the most successful companies in the world.

The main difficulties

The main difficulties facing British SMEs in Japan are grouped below under four key headings: high costs, recruitment problems, market restrictions and government-related obstacles. On the whole they are more a product of the toughness of the Japanese market and the so-called system of 'cooperative' competition that exists between Japanese firms, rather than 'unfair competition' or 'restrictive practices', although these do exist. For new firms this means a substantially greater investment in time and money is required, compared to other overseas markets, to develop local ties, build a market presence and adapt internal management practices to organise and motivate employees. However, recent changes in Japan, reviewed in Chapter 2 and summarised at the end of this book, mean that the difficulties described here no longer represent the insurmountable barriers they once did.

High costs of start-up and operation in Japan

First and foremost, particularly for SMEs, Japan is an expensive place to live and work. At an exchange rate of 100 Yen to the US Dollar (a long-broken 'ceiling') Japanese prices are 84 percent higher than the average for other OECD countries. Most manufacturing costs are now the highest in the world, including sites, water, electricity, construction costs, shipping costs and so on, all except interest rates. The cost of labour in manufacturing is more than double that of the UK, with hourly earnings in 1993 in Japan at $20.48 compared to $9.29 in Britain (although in terms of days lost to industrial disputes companies in Japan lose about a third of the UK number). Other business costs are also high. The 'real tax burden' for companies in Japan (according to the Keidaneren) is 48.8 percent compared to 32.6 percent in the USA and 19.5 percent in the UK and the withholding tax on dividends remitted from Japan overseas is unusually high (JETRO, 1995).

Beyond this, establishing a presence in Japan is expensive from the start. Before setting up a local office managers must expect to pay for lengthy trips by senior representatives to assess local markets and meet with customers, distributors, sales organisations, sub-contractors and so on, to establish senior-level contacts.

During the set-up period for the firms sampled the costs of land and property and therefore office space were a heavy constraint. The real estate market was notoriously inflexible and large deposits (which tie-up large amounts of capital permanently), plus non-returnable 'key-money' and restrictive terms for rental accommodation made office space difficult to find and very expensive (peak monthly rental was about £630 per *tsubo* - 3.3m² - in the central wards of Tokyo before 1991)(Huddlestone, 1990). With a slide in Tokyo's property market, linked to the current economic recession, this situation has eased considerably. In fact land prices have fallen each year since 1991 and there have been particularly heavy falls in the cost of commercial property (down 11.3 percent in 1993, 10 percent in 1994 and over 6 percent in 1995)(Baker, 1995). This has added to the financial instability, since property is so widely used as collateral to back loans and investments, but it represents a good opportunity for newcomers, especially since property rents have fallen at least as fast as property prices. Property prices in Tokyo, however, are still far higher (up to three times) than their equivalent in London or New York. Heavy taxes on the sale of land maintain an a highly illiquid property market.

Having emphasised the high costs of property in Tokyo it is worth mentioning a key advantage of the Japanese system compared to the UK that a number of firms cited. The average length of property lease in Tokyo is around two years and this allows foreign firms to remain fairly flexible in their office location. SMEs can therefore adjust their monthly property costs, their in-house facilities and their proximity to customers, distributors or services relatively quickly, according to their evolving size, profitability and business focus.

Also in the context of the high cost of office space it is worth noting how certain central business locations are highly valued because of the kudos and image they portray for a company, particularly by the fact that it can afford such a location. This effect, particularly in Tokyo, is seen to be far greater than in say London or New York where office rents are also linked to central location, desirability and image. Because of the historical respectability of property-ownership in Japan expensive offices with large reception areas are an indication that a firm has invested in a long-term presence.

Although property prices having been coming down for some time now, overheads, such as fax and telephone lines, equipment costs and translation costs, remain expensive. The cost of warehousing, for example, is about 20 times that of the US (hence the strong impetus for 'just-in-time' delivery systems). The basic cost of living in Japan is also very expensive, with Tokyo the most expensive city in the world (175, with London as a base of 100 and the second most expensive city, Geneva at 132, using an index of housing and living expenses compiled by PE-International) (Donkin, 1995). Managers responsible for setting up the office should convey real costs at an early stage to senior management and get full support before making long-term investments.

Following a study in 1990 the US Department of Commerce estimated the costs for the first year of operation for a 4-person office in Tokyo's central business district at 40-46 million Yen (now around £250,000), not including costs for expatriate staff. Most companies examined in their study had grossly underestimated these costs.

Although the labour market in Japan has also eased for foreign firms (discussed below) Japanese employees are still expensive relative to UK staff, with regular bonuses added to already high salaries. If UK representatives are sent to Japan on expatriate packages this also adds considerably to costs. One manager estimated a minimum of £100,000 to keep one person from UK in Japan for a year.

One executive opening up a one-man branch office in Tokyo for his small firm recounted a list of practical start-up costs that made their market entry more expensive than anticipated. To rent a dual office and apartment it was normal in Japan to be asked for one-month's rent as deposit and a further month's rent as 'key money' (non-returnable), plus between 5 and 7 month's rent as a lump sum up-front. Most landlords also require a foreigner to have a local guarantor, financial backer or personal reference, because of the uncertain status of visas. Most newcomers arrive on tourist visas which are limited to three months. A full working visa can be difficult to obtain and, in the case of a manager for a new foreign enterprise may depend on proof of the financial status of the company and an indication that the firm will employ Japanese personnel.

In addition to these expenses the costs of keeping a manager in Tokyo permanently and the costs of running even a small office are higher than anywhere else. This includes services and transport costs, for example, a minimum essential entertainment allowance and translation costs for documentation and corporate material, much of which should be entirely customised for Japan. A new phone line, for instance, costs just over £500, which has given rise in Tokyo to an informal market for personal numbers, freed when people move apartments.

Putting a realistic figure on start-up costs and the likely time-scale before profits begin to show is the first key objective for SMEs considering the Japanese market.

A major contributing factor to high start-up costs in Japan is the long time it takes before new firms begin to turn over business. Most interviewees suggested 3-5 years before a new business would start to show a profit (although recently there have been stories of foreign firms finding 'instant success' in Japan). Obviously this varies by sector and product but a clear message from both new and experienced managers was that success in Japan required a great deal of commitment and patience over a long period of time to gain acceptance from local customers and firms. For both individual managers and their firms reputation is paramount in Japan. The saying to 'sit on the stone' was quoted by several interviewees to describe the testing period most foreign firms undergo before Japanese companies and customers will establish ties. It takes longer in Japan partly because relationships are traditionally set-up for the long-term rather than being based on temporary, price-led transactions.

Local recruitment difficulties

The labour shortage for foreign firms in Japan was particularly acute before the current recession. Not only were both the labour surplus and labour mobility very low but the majority of Japanese employees did not regard employment by a foreign company as either secure or particularly 'respectable'. Although these factors are now changing, with the deterioration of lifetime employment in Japan and the 'internationalisation' of younger members of the workforce, they still present major problems. In fact, an interview-based survey of 'obstacles to business activities of foreign firms in Japan', conducted in 1994 still put 'difficulties in securing manpower' at the top of its list (JETRO, 1995).

Skilled Japanese managers, engineers, technicians and sales people, experienced in a specialist field, with some knowledge of English and a willingness to work for foreign companies were especially scarce 5-10 years ago and are still in short supply. It is also difficult for Westerners to judge the quality of Japanese candidates particularly when, as one respondent put it, 'the unusual Japanese are the easiest employees for foreign firms to attract'. Foreign firms are still very unlikely to attract the 'cream' from the elite universities such as Tokyo, Hitotsubashi and Kyoto.

Although larger firms use headhunters for senior staff and can offer high salaries both options are too expensive for most SMEs. Managers suggested various ways of finding and attracting suitable Japanese employees. To track down suitable, new employees it is advisable to plug into as many relevant networks as possible via existing Japanese contacts in distribution companies, competitors or allied foreign firms in the relevant sector. This also provides a route for making the initial approach to a potential employee, via a known intermediary, as is the Japanese way, rather than 'cold' recruitment. If possible it is also beneficial to develop ties with local universities and specific university departments, which is how most large Japanese companies do their recruiting.

In order to retain existing employees as well as attract new blood firms must also address at least some of the problems faced by the Japanese that are willing to work for a foreign company. The main drawbacks are to do with security and image. Security of employment and guaranteed advancement up an age-related hierarchy have long been well-known (though perhaps exaggerated) strengths of larger Japanese firms. They also offer a 'social' guarantee for employees in terms of the image or reputation of the company in which each employee shares. Foreign companies must be aware of these benefits, which especially apply to the more experienced staff they seek, and strive to enhance the attractiveness of their company vis-a-vis the competing options. To maintain stability within the organisation expatriate managers are also advised, where possible, to develop senior Japanese managers in-house and bring them up through the firm rather than bringing in outsiders which disrupts the organisation of the work place for existing employees.

One manager, now head of a 28-employee SME, registered in Japan and operating in the construction industry, took the view that the fate of his firm rested in the hands of his employees and used this his guiding principle for hiring, organising and motivating his employees. As an independent start-up his success or failure was determined by the quality of his almost exclusively Japanese workforce and his relationship with them. His main advantage in coping with the recruitment problem came from his own experience studying at a Japanese university for six years and his knowledge of the Japanese language and culture (although his self-confessed weak point, and one that almost led to the collapse of his business, was his lack of knowledge about the business-side of Japan when he began the process of establishing his firm).

Most Japanese firms recruit direct from colleges and universities in a traditional annual round of recruitment drives wherein certain firms have long-standing relationships with certain universities or departments and expect a number of graduates (sometimes earmarked well in advance of their graduation) to join them. With an informal network of colleagues in specialist university departments that matched the needs of his company, this manager was able to pick up the highest quality staff for his firm. He also ran a holiday work experience scheme for students, giving him the chance to test their abilities and giving them the chance to work in his company, without a long-term commitment to stay. Regarding recruitment, he described Japan as a 'village society' where informal contacts and established networks are essential, both for information on good prospective employees, but also for 'advertising' what a firm has to offer a potential recruit.

In addition to this he realised from his knowledge of Japanese society that a major problem for potential Japanese employees is the lack of job security offered by foreign firms. For most Japanese the evidence for this is the hire-and-fire activities of non-Japanese companies in their own countries, as well as in Japan. It is imperative that foreign companies counteract this reputation to attract the best staff. Moreover, this is as much a matter of image-management as the introduction of real job security in terms of long-term contracts and generous pensions schemes.

Japanese employees (particularly senior managers) are wary of joining foreign firm subsidiaries or working under a foreign boss partly because they lack control over the success or failure of the overall operation and therefore over their own future. They cannot assess the level of commitment, to employees and to staying in the Japanese market, of those in control of the operation as easily as they can in a Japanese firm. Foreign managers wanting to recruit and retain the best Japanese employees must emphasise these aspects of their firm far more than they would elsewhere.

This owner-manager did this primarily through setting up a junior partner system, where part-ownership in the firm was offered to the best employees after a minimum of three years employment. This acted as an incentive mechanism while also providing security and a reciprocal commitment from the company to the employee. A bonus scheme of up to 150 percent of salary added to the incentive scheme and, in contrast to the archetypal Japanese firm, the promotion hierarchy was not rigidly age-related.

There are other difficulties beyond those related to job-security. For example, various special problems can affect the hiring and management of Japanese women employees. Women make up 40 percent of the Japanese workforce but make on average 60 percent of male wages. This is a growing source of friction in the workplace and is providing added impetus to changing patterns of employment. On the one hand the traditional, shy, so-called 'office lady' who lacks confidence but follows orders to the letter is unlikely to want to work for a foreign company, particularly a small one, particularly in direct contact with foreign males. On the other hand there are a growing number of the 'new breed' of women worker in Japan, both at the secretarial level but also in management, that are attracted to the relative independence of working for a foreign firm. This is seen to be a step away from at least some of the discrimination they face in the more traditional Japanese firms. The women that make it to the top in Japan tend to be leagues ahead of their male colleagues and should often be targeted in recruitment (although this is not true for all sectors of the economy or all managerial roles).

For many foreign SMEs overcoming the difficulties of attracting good staff and retaining them is achieved by taking on a Japanese manager in the most senior position at the local office. Someone who is already well-connected in the industry, someone who can organise the office according to Japanese business practices and someone who can assure would-be employees of the good-intentions and good reputation of the foreign employer and the long-term stability of the Japan-based operation is the best person for the job.

Market restrictions

Although restrictions on market access lies at the centre of the on-going international trade talks, primarily between the US and Japan, actual barriers to market entry are often difficult to identify and vary considerably by sector and product. Moreover, a point often missed by outside interests currently applying pressure on the Japanese government to open its markets is that Japan's ministries, despite their influential bureaucracies, have very little direct control (and far less than in the past) over many sectors of the economy. Political pressure will only have an influence in the areas where government regulations are responsible for the limited foreign participation in local markets. These are, for example, the construction industry, telecommunications (e.g. the battle over Motorola's cellular phones, used by the Clinton administration in an attempt to force a deregulation of NTT's monopoly) and a number of service sectors, such as the insurance market and the legal profession.

In the sectors that actually account for the bulk of material trade, such as cars and car components, electronics, computers and software, chemicals and most consumer products a large proportion of market restrictions are beyond the government's direct control. Although in some of these sectors bureaucratic regulations, testing requirements and over-complex documentation are cited as non-tariff barriers the actual difficulties of enforcing quantitative limits on the private sector in Japan to boost imports do not seem to be recognised

In the light of this it was to be expected that the sample companies reported very different problems with market access, according to their sectors of operation. However, more important to most companies than government limitations, save those involved in the construction industry, were the *informal infrastructures governing their markets and the form of 'cooperative competition' that characterises the behaviour of Japanese firms.* These made it more difficult for foreign companies, particularly newcomers, to become established or expand their markets in Japan.

'Tied' market systems, based on informal business relationships and corporate networks, are common to all global economies (especially in developing countries), in varying degrees. In Japan they are particularly strong and centre on long-standing relationships between firms that are members of *dango* and *keiretsu* - type families. Industry associations and other corporate 'clubs' serve as meeting points (or network nodes) wherein consensus between members, which include distributors, sub-contractors and often banks as well as the major manufacturers, can be formalised. A large number of the regulations that newcomers to a specific market have to adhere to come from these organisations. They may have influential representatives from various government ministries as members but they are privately funded and directed (see the description earlier in Chapter 2).

> The story of one firm illustrates this point. This is a small manufacturer and exporter of slot machines, such as rides for children, which are common in the UK but less common in Japan. The company has around 65 employees in the UK and 10 in a sales and assembly operation in Japan, with total firm turnover of about £19 million. Their entry into Japan was prompted by the fact that all types of food and drinks dispensers existed in Japan, as did the

famous '*pachinko*' parlours, but the market was ripe for a more diversified range of games-related slot-machines. The anticipated market opportunity in Japan was very large with a domestic capacity approaching an estimated 3 million of this company's type of machines compared to the UK's 250,000 installed machines.

Despite having a long-standing link with Japan and some experience exporting and importing components this firm had never before tried to import, customise and sell full machines in Japan. Although it came upon some initial resistance from the existing companies that it had done business with in the past (now direct competitors) this did not represent a serious impediment. A major stumbling block was that it had to become a member of the local industry association to be legally allowed to sell or manufacture its products in Japan. After being discouraged from applying for membership by existing members and local competitors the firm also found itself prevented from doing business with other Japanese firms because of the power of the association, effectively acting as a cartel of interest groups.

The government authority responsible for monitoring the sales and use of slot machines in Japan, and for applying various regulations pertaining to manufacturers, was closely tied to the industry association. They had the power to prevent market entry by applying various restrictions on specific companies, ranging from the direct barring of firms that do not manufacture in Japan, to indirect measures, such as delays in testing safety standards on imports or requiring convoluted Japanese documentation alongside sales. These kinds of measures are surprisingly common across a range of sectors and make up the bulk of non-tariff barriers restricting imports into Japan.

The power of the government authority was combined with the influence of industry members who were able, for example, to limit existing sales of certain of the firms products by putting pressure on 'tied' retailers and distributors, blocking the standard outlets and distribution channels. The cohesive nature of some industry groups allows them to place strong enough pressure on suppliers, retailers and customers that foreign products will fail to break into the market even if they are substantially cheaper.

Only after several years of negotiation was the firm eventually accepted as the first non-Japanese member of the association. This procedure still involved a visit to its manufacturing facilities in the UK by association officials, because a certain level of manufacturing capability had to be demonstrated before membership was granted. Plus, some behind-the-scenes lobbying from the British Embassy in Tokyo was also eventually necessary. A requirement for joining this particular association was also for the firm to incorporate certain hardware manufactured locally by a Japanese member into its products, ensuring it became more closely linked to the group.

In many cases these long-standing semi-formal barriers set up by protective private sector interests are the most difficult to crack. If the dominant group is united in their opposition to new competition members of these informal 'cartels' may bring similar market pressure to bear on those Japanese firms that assist foreign entrants or establish joint ventures with overseas firms. But the managing director interviewed in the UK felt that the key lesson they had learnt about Japan was that many market 'regulations' and restrictions are untested or flexible according to the pressure exerted by 'outsiders' and the perseverance with which it is exerted. A significant advantage is gained by understanding who are the main influential players within these informal Japanese 'consortia' and what are the 'in-house' rules and regulations governing their behaviour. This kind of preparation is invaluable before deciding on a negotiating stance or a strategy for entering the market.

As important an impediment as industry groups are the multi-layered distribution and retail networks which SMEs in particular find difficult to bypass. These were described in Chapter 2 which provided some background to these aspects of the Japanese economy. As stated earlier, it is common for a producer to have to deal with 8 or more different regional distributors each with three or more levels of wholesaler below them dividing the market by product or sub-region before reaching the retailer and finally the consumer. This large number of middlemen is the main reason behind the excessively high prices charged to the final consumer. Moreover, the distance that this creates between the producer and the final consumer creates a considerable dependence on established trading and distribution companies, giving them sustainable leverage in the market.

The 'tied' or long-term sub-contractor relationships that are also a well-known feature of Japan's domestic economy favour existing suppliers and particularly corporate 'family' members. Foreign SMEs that are new to the market and are not known to large Japanese firms are least likely to be taken on as sub-contractors.

A final market 'restriction' worth mentioning are the 'patriotic' preferences of the average Japanese consumer and, perhaps, the average Japanese middle-manager responsible for company purchasing policy. The Japanese simply prefer Japanese products (as do consumers in many countries), seeing them as reliable, high quality and innovative. Although these preferences are changing in the current economic environment newcomers will find these constraints still set Japan apart from other overseas markets.

How do British SMEs overcome these market restrictions? In all these cases there was a significant variation in the fortunes of existing companies (and therefore the potential success of new enterprises) according to the product and service offered. Niche products and services that have no local competition, like those based on a new innovation or, for example, British design skills, have the best chance as they will meet limited resistance from the Japanese side. Indeed they are actively looked for by Japanese trading companies who will earn high profits from certain products that are new to Japan.

A common strategy for most firms was to 'Japanize' their products as much as possible to have greater appeal to local consumers. In some cases this went to extremes as a purely cosmetic measure with some firms locally re-packaging imported goods that were not adapted in any way, to reach the customer as 'Japanese' manufactures.

An important consideration for SMEs that were forced to go through the convoluted distribution hierarchy was to develop a close relationship with agents in the field and build up a first-hand understanding about customer requirements. This allows the firm to adapt its products and its marketing more effectively rather than relying on sales agents to take on these responsibilities. Another option is to establish a direct sales and support force tied to your own operations. Despite the expense and the inherent difficulties of building a customer network from scratch, this route appears to be the best option for some products, particularly those needing a lot of technical after-sales support.

In terms of the constraints coming from industry associations the best advice from managers was to be aware of the power of such groups, join them and make Japanese contacts within them whenever possible. Beyond that the options for bypassing their influence is often limited.

In recent years, since the start of the recession, there have been a number of significant changes in Japan's industrial groupings and distribution infrastructure, marked by a general loosening of ties and an increasingly price-led retail and distribution mechanism. As discussed, the opportunities for foreign companies and imported products in Japan are more widespread now than at any time in the past as a result of these changes.

Government-related obstacles

The preceding section shows how non-tariff barriers, beyond the control of the Japanese government, restrict access to Japan's markets for foreign firms and British SMEs. Japan also has considerably more government regulations on business than most countries and this excessive intervention is made more difficult by the lack of transparency in some areas of economic activity. As mentioned, government-related obstacles are prominent in certain industry sectors and, according to the managers interviewed, also affect other aspects of a foreign company's activities.

The construction industry is one of the most prominent examples, and one where British companies in Japan are fairly heavily involved. 4 sample companies were directly involved in the construction industry and several others sold certain product lines to local construction companies. It is a sector where very strong corporate groups (*dangos*) in the private sector combine with 'fixed' project tendering and procurement practices in the public sector to create a highly organised 'imperfect' market favouring Japanese companies over foreign ones (Japanese construction companies are also known as the '*gumis*', or construction 'gangs' as in Shimizu-gumi, Kumigai-gumi or Kajima-gumi, which some say denotes a troop or battalion). The case-studies contain details of the problems faced specifically by SMEs and their experiences are supported by other sources. Because of the media focus on the problems of market access in this sector these are fully documented elsewhere (Baxter, 1993). The survey experience shows for instance that price is usually not a consideration for the purchasing of construction materials, so British imports, though cheaper will tend not to be 'competitive'. The more successful SMEs in this sector are in niche markets, offering materials, designs or expertise that are not offered by Japanese firms.

There are other sectors where the Japanese government has a strong involvement in the private sector and where a change in government procurement practices or regulations would open up the market for foreign firms. Many of these have been the subject of trade talks at the senior political level. Telecommunications (a \$9 billion a-year market), where the Japanese company NTT (the largest company in the world by market capitalisation) is effectively a government-supported monopoly, is a sector heavily influenced by government procurement practices and standards enforcement. The medical equipment sector, controlled through hospital purchasing restrictions, is also relatively closed to foreign firms. Both of these, together with the insurance, flat glass and the vehicles and vehicle parts sectors were the subject of US-Japan trade negotiations in 1994 (Nakamoto and Abrahams, 1994; Dunne, 1994).

Across a much broader range of sectors Japanese government regulations also affect foreign companies importing products into Japan and adapting these for the local market. A number of these were no worse than those that exist in other global markets. More serious a restriction, though highly variable across product groups, was the red tape and regulatory complexities governing imports of particular products, including local testing requirements (often different from international standards), complex documentation and various unnecessary delays.

Local knowledge amongst experienced SME managers goes a long way in helping bypass many of these inconveniences. Re-classifying imports or bringing in goods via one route rather than another, providing certain technical documents or applying for licenses from one department rather than another can all smooth the process. This does, however, add to the already long learning curve for new managers establishing themselves in Japan.

One manager of his own small import and distribution company had severe difficulties with licenses when he first began his business in Japan. To operate as an importer, wholesaler and retailer, covering the entire chain 'from dock to shop', he required three different licenses. This was treated with suspicion by the various officials responsible because it was unusual for a small company. His application was blocked for some time by a barrage of detailed questions and form-filling, made more difficult because he was new to Japan and did not speak Japanese.

This manager was eventually able to get all three licenses, with considerable help from other, more experienced British SME owner-managers. From them he learned the importance of understanding some of the subtleties of the 'double-speak' used by bureaucrats. Only rarely are there straightforward 'yes' or 'no' answers or 'black' or 'white' situations (true to form for most interaction with Japanese, but a more pronounced aspect of interaction with government officials). Most of the time the foreign manager is swimming in a sea of ambiguity when dealing with Japanese officialdom. Knowing how to speak their language (as well as basic Japanese), how to work around problem areas and how not to cause offence or long-term disagreement is the key.

Beyond trade-related problems many SME managers complained about a general degree of uncertainty in the interpretation of legislation regarding foreign companies by different Japanese government agencies. Examples include tax status problems, employee rights, legal rights of expatriate managers and so on. It many cases it was suggested that the problem lay with junior bureaucrats in various local government bodies who were unsure of how to categorise or deal with foreigners and foreign companies and chose to cloud rather than clarify certain issues to avoid taking responsibility. The bureaucratic 'officialdom' at the middle and lower-level civil service was said by many interviewees to be highly 'risk averse' and consistently failed to take the initiative to remove barriers in the way of foreigners and their business activities.

Taxes are a good example of this. In Japan there is a high level of corporation tax (described earlier in this chapter) compared to the UK level. This varies in relation to a number of factors, including the registered status of the office and, reportedly, the residency status of the owner or manager. Tax auditing is carried out at the local level and is the responsibility of the ward office in which a company is located. According to the managers interviewed, this gives rise to significant variations in how taxes are assessed and how well or thoroughly they are assessed, depending on which ward the business is located in. Much of this variation results from the tax auditors in different ward offices having very different levels of experience dealing with foreign companies. (The Japanese accounting system is also fundamentally different from international accounting).

On top of this, foreign company managers argued, the tax laws applied to foreign companies are unnecessarily vague and subject to different interpretations by different officers, making it difficult to assess how taxes will affect sales and income over the long-term. Although the Japanese Government has reduced tax rates for SMEs some companies reported having to pay higher taxes because they were foreign companies.

Beyond corporation tax (*'hojin zei'*), income tax (*'shotoku zei'*), there is consumption tax (*'shohi zei'*) and various taxes on inheritance and gifts, and a local enterprise tax. These are the assorted responsibility of the Ministry of Finance, the National Tax Administration Agency, the Regional Tax Office and the District Tax Office.

A number of respondents described the Japanese taxation system as 'informal', compared to the UK system, in that a certain amount of flexibility was built-in to allow movement between category headings and between tax years. This enabled small companies to avoid excessive tax on revenue and profits which was necessary for financial survival. Any 'flexibility' in Japanese business regulations would seem to be entirely out of character but this arrangement is apparently accepted by the authorities because it gives them considerable power over both local and foreign SMEs to encourage them to toe the line in other respects. This is partly necessary because officially the number of years for carrying over tax losses in Japan is much shorter than in Western countries.

Another common and yet apparently unnecessary problem, that affected only foreign firms, concerned visas. Non-Japanese interviewees frequently complained that visas were often difficult to get and took a long time to process. Many managers had begun work in Japan on tourist visas because of these difficulties, requiring them to leave and return every three months. Others, particularly the small firm owner-managers had taken up other jobs locally (like teaching English) to get temporary work visas and establish themselves in various networks. Without a visa it can be very difficult to get a telephone or rent office space or employ Japanese staff.

The inconvenient, even unnecessary, alien registration and re-entry visa regulations create obstacles even for foreign managers who have been in Japan for some time. Many managers believed there was a need for the UK government, perhaps via the embassy, to push for clarification of the rights and requirements of British subjects based in Japan.

Some interviewees blamed the more senior levels of the local bureaucracies in Japan (the general policy makers), rather than the lower, ward-level officials (who deal with day-to-day matters), for this kind of problem. One suggested that the most senior decision-makers in the Ministry of Justice were responsible for making things difficult for foreign firms, particularly foreign SMEs, in Japan. This was done by tying visa applications for foreign company presidents in red tape and by requiring high levels of capital and annual sales before foreign firms could be registered locally.

Finally under this heading it is worth mentioning that restrictive government bureaucracies also hinder the operations of Japanese firms and deregulation within the domestic economy is strongly sought by Japanese companies who are now pulling away from government controls at every level. The Keidanren is particularly active in calling for a freeing up of the economy including for instance the removal of import tariffs for car parts (Keidanren, 1993). Any Japanese retailer wishing to open a supermarket must read 17 laws and 45 administrative regulations, fill in 200 pages of application forms and wait up to 18 months for a government response (Dawkins and Thomson, 1993). Whether permission is granted or not may depend more on the government connections fostered by local competitors than market demand.

To sum up then, the main difficulties facing managers in Japan come under one or a combination of: high costs, problems recruiting and keeping good local staff, a variety of market access restrictions, and problems stemming from the influence or requirements of the Japanese government. Part of the process of overcoming these difficulties and being successful in Japan requires foreign managers to attempt to bridge the cultural divide between themselves and their employees, customers, suppliers and other Japanese organisations that they rely on or come into contact with. This is the task facing any manager working in an international, multi-cultural business environment in any overseas market. However, the mis-interpretation and mis-communication that can arise in Japan can be far more damaging to the successful management of a local enterprise than in most foreign markets because of the enormous differences between the business cultures.

Management/mis-management problems

The significant language, cultural and behavioural differences between the Japanese and 'Westerners' complicate interaction at all levels. Problems arising from these differences are not wholly down to the inexperience of managers in new foreign corporate entrants. It is important to remember that the vast majority of Japanese companies (most of them SMEs) have either none or a limited number of operations based abroad and, moreover, a large number of Japanese managers have never travelled to the West. They may well lack experience of joint-ventures, alliances or agreements with foreign companies and their initial resistance (if encountered) may stem from unfamiliarity rather than prejudice.

This section will look at a variety of management problems that tend to affect foreign firms in Japan, partly as a result of these cultural differences and partly a result of differences in the way the Japanese conduct business and manage inter-company relations. The following will focus on (1) internal office problems; (2) misunderstandings between UK head offices and their subsidiaries in Japan, and; (3) difficulties experienced by UK managers with Japanese firms in Japan.

Internal office problems

Previous examples above have shown the need for foreign managers in Japan to adapt their work practices and conditions of employment to recruit and retain the best Japanese employees. Further changes are necessary to organise and motivate the local workforce to maximise their commitment to the company and the overall efficiency of the local operation.

In the immediate workplace Japanese employees are used to different forms of office organisation than Westerners. Managers' experience suggested that in general installing a Japanese style of management made employees more motivated, committed and effective in their jobs. Generic characteristics include a structured office hierarchy with clear lines of command (usually based on seniority and involving specific job-titles), decision-making by committee (in keeping with *'ringi'* , *'nemawashi'* or consensus-based policy making), clearly-defined office rules, clearly-defined targets and procedures for each area of responsibility and also more specific contract provisions covering bonus schemes, pensions, hiring and firing procedures and so on. When the company is organised in this fashion foreign managers are also expected to behave in a certain way, with both staff and customers. Both respond better if foreigners have a certain degree of knowledge and empathy with local traditions and culture, rather than enforcing their own style.

The above characteristics may seem like side-issues for many managers but they are given a high priority in Japanese companies and are essential if a foreign company wants to attract and effectively organise Japanese employees. What they do is provide a recognisable structure, familiar guidelines and roles in an explicit hierarchy, giving Japanese employees confidence in their employer and a degree of security. It also shows a commitment to doing (some) things the 'local way' and implies a commitment to a long-term presence in Japan.

In some of the sample companies early failures and slow starts could be traced back directly to internal personnel problems, low morale, high staff turnover or poor communications that prevented the firm getting on with its main functions efficiently and effectively. In some cases the problem was the result of a poor *selection* of Japanese staff, mainly by inexperienced British managers setting up a base in Japan without the contacts or expertise to hire the best available local personnel (a common criticism of past management, rather than an honest admission regarding current problems by an existing administration!).

Contrary to the stereotypical view of the Japanese, employees can and do vary a great deal and can cause management difficulties even when local styles of organisation are adopted. One company we studied experienced a range of problems with personnel throughout its early years, arising from a combination of inexperience, poor management and (in retrospect) bad luck!

The first manager, whose responsibility it was to establish the initial outlet for this British manufacturing SME in Japan, for customising and selling industrial printing equipment, had a number of difficulties with Japanese staff, despite running a relatively small local office. Although it is not easy to tell whether these stemmed from his poor choice of personnel (he did not speak Japanese and was new to Japan), from poor advice from colleagues, or simply from bad luck, his experience showed that it is a mistake to organise Japanese employees on the basis of the stereotypical views of them commonly held in the West (honest, loyal, hard-working and so on). Although the Japanese are probably less heterogeneous than other nationalities they obviously still vary a great deal as individuals and, as mentioned above, foreign firms often attract the 'less average' or more unusual employees.

This manager described significant problems with his local employees from the outset, including drinking during working hours in the office and absenteeism, as well as numerous 'failures of communication' relating to the poor performance of specific staff members. He had particular difficulties with one secretary who continually requested increases in her salary and who resigned and subsequently returned to work on several occasions. He also had a complicated and long-running battle with a fraudulent accountant who was found to be creaming a small proportion of profits from the company's accounts and who turned out to have some very wealthy and influential relatives, who became involved when the managing director decided to take legal steps to recover company funds.

The British manager had some advice for new foreign managers regarding Japanese employees, gained from his unusually problematic start-up in Japan. He stressed above all that, contrary to his initial perceptions (and those of many other foreign managers), Japanese employees require constant checking and monitoring to ensure each allocated task is carried out as ordered. Compared to employees elsewhere the Japanese tended to be 'risk averse' and often showed surprisingly little initiative and a great deal of dependence on senior management, he suggested.

He also emphasised the importance of the office regulations requirements in Japan which foreign managers should understand thoroughly to avoid being taken advantage of. The requirement is that every office in Japan with more than 10 employees should have a written document, the 'Rules of Employment' (from Article 89 of the Labour Standards Law) listing the rules governing all the conditions of employment, from general conduct, confidentiality clauses, responsibilities, reprimands and bonuses and so on. A standard format is provided by the authorities and is customised for specific businesses. The key thing is that these are constantly referred to and updated in the running of the business and act as a guideline for personnel matters. A foreign boss that does not know of their contents (or even their existence) is setting the stage for major problems with Japanese staff. Japan is not a legalistic society (in the way the USA is) but it is a society of rules and they are expected to be understood by everyone.

Rather than signing a contract when they are employed office workers very often take an oath (and often sign a written version) that they will abide by the office regulations pertaining to their new place of work. These may describe for example which workplace transgressions require a written apology from the employee and which will result in docked pay or a period of suspension without pay. Likewise they stipulate the levels of bonuses, prize money, 'congratulatory money' and 'condolence money' that employees can expect from their company. The British manager responsible for setting up the Japan office had not taken on board the central function of these documents and the above initiation process for new employees until relatively late in the process and the internal workplace problems were partly a result of this.

In addition to the internal office difficulties described this manager (experienced and used to working abroad through he was) also failed to develop appropriate relationships with major customers. Key contacts were left to sales-people to nurture and, without direct support from the most senior manager, many did not last long. A legal battle over technical patents with a major local competitor (a minefield for many SMEs without recourse to internal legal experts) was also handled badly. Not that the initial suit was the British manager's fault, only that he chose to fight the contest very publicly, damaging the company's local reputation (even though it was in the right).

This first manager did not entirely fail in his efforts, and did provide the company with a reasonable initial base in Japan. The most senior managers back in the UK, however, decided a change was necessary and placed an experienced Japanese manager in charge of the operation. In retrospect they made the right strategic choice but picked the wrong man for the job, and a range of new problems began. In particular the Japanese manager embarked on a series of major changes without the consent of headquarters staff. After numerous battles over the control of the Japan office he was replaced by a younger Japanese manager with substantial experience working with Western firms.

Subsequent interviews in the same company but with different managers over several years (including a discussion at head office with the UK managing director) have shown that this firm has overcome various difficulties and start-up problems in Japan to eventually carve itself a successful niche in a very competitive overseas market. The overall firm now employ's just over 500 people in the UK. It had set up an office in Tokyo in 1989 with one British manager and around 10 local staff and, when last visited, the firm was employing between 15 local staff, plus numerous sales personnel, and commanded about 13 percent of the Japanese market for its products. It had a local turnover of more than £3 million after experiencing a growth rate of 20 percent over 1992 and 1993.

Two false starts, one a joint venture with a large local manufacturer and the second a tie-up with a distributor both failed, before the final option of a locally-registered company (a 'KK') was chosen.

The firm initially expected too much return, too quickly from far too little investment in its Japanese operation, but constant exchange visits and the gradual accumulation of knowledge about Japan's unique problems for foreigners have since reaped some local market successes against Japanese giants such as Toshiba and Hitachi. All involved agreed that working continuously on personnel issues and building strong UK-Japan management and employee relationships underlies its eventual success.

For many firms, particularly those with larger Japan offices, a common problem lay in effectively integrating British and Japanese managers and employees within an agreed organisational structure. Difficulties associated with poorly integrated management groups, stemming from cultural clashes, mixed loyalties, incompatible work practices, mis-trust and so on, often affected new ventures for far longer than anticipated by head office. The above example shows how important it is to understand the routine guidelines and protocol expected by Japanese employees and work colleagues and how important it is to invest time and effort from the beginning to establish a mutually-agreed mode of operation. Without this, neither Japanese or British managers will be motivated or committed towards the long-term success of the venture.

One common problem experienced by senior British managers, for example, was with middle-management, the so-called '*kacho*-level'. In Japanese companies, once consensus has been reached through discussion at all relevant levels over a particular problem or a new initiative, middle managers will tend to take the lead in implementing the agreed solution. This very often conflicts with the hands-on approach of Western managers who are themselves used to making day-to-day operational decisions. To avoid a damaging overlap in the allocation of responsibilities senior British managers must make it very clear from the start which level of management will take charge of which tasks.

Another difficulty frequently cited by respondents stemmed from 'reward' payments, bonuses and promotion. In the Japanese management system it can be difficult to reward individuals because all promotions and payments, including the standard, yearly bonuses, tend to be geared directly to the number of years of service and an employee's level in the company hierarchy. British managers expressed frustration at the fact that this makes it difficult to motivate staff in the way they are used to doing, or establish the basic elements of a meritocracy. In many cases managers established some form of bonus or incentive scheme that combined the Japanese and Western systems.

Smaller foreign firms can have particular difficulties attracting and holding on to good secretaries, partly because there are too few Japanese middle managers (or none) to act as go-betweens. Evidence from two firms included in the survey suggest that local secretaries may have poor English (or a lack of confidence in using their English on a daily basis) and may find the prospect of translation work a barrier to employment. Some said there was also something of a fear of foreign bosses, and young women often had considerable problems communicating and discussing work problems with foreign males.

Similarly, some Japanese managers may find it very difficult to work with foreign bosses and need to have clear lines of responsibility and regular interaction with British counterparts to maintain an 'explicit' working relationship. Another case study example further emphasises these points.

A young British manager, now managing director in charge of a 10-person printing office in Japan affiliated to a larger London-based company, described the problems experienced in the early stages of setting up the Japan operation. He had been taken on under a more senior British manager in the early stages because he had several years experience in Japan and could speak the language. The latter had no experience of living or working in Japan and as a direct result immediately had a number of difficulties managing both the in-house Japanese staff and managing an alliance that the firm had set up with a Japanese printing house to ease the initial market entry process.

The first serious problem was actually finding good staff. The senior manager could not speak Japanese and had no contacts in the relevant informal networks through which, in Japan more than in most countries, the hiring of specialists takes place. The company therefore began almost immediately with the disadvantage of relatively poor staff. These are difficult to fire and impossible to 'let go' without prejudicing other good employees against working for a particular foreign company.

The senior British manager, in charge of the office, also failed to establish clear lines of responsibility and seniority within the office from the beginning. This problem was compounded by the hiring of a senior Japanese manager to handle the 'Japanese side' of the organisation, including links with local suppliers and customers. Head office in London were undecided as to whether to make the Japanese manager the second-in-command, or place him third in the office hierarchy, below the young British manager, in the early stages of setting up the office. This decision would determine who would be in charge of the branch after the senior British manager returned to UK and should have been settled at the earliest possible moment. The confusion left the new Japanese staff uncertain as to their own position in the small internal hierarchy and also uncertain as to who was the most senior manager, a far more serious problem in Japan than is anticipated by newcomers.

The inexperience of the senior British manager and his failure to master Japanese caused other problems, related to his lack of understanding of how to run a Japanese office. These were added to by the fact that he relied on a limited number of Japanese staff who could speak good English - they, not often best at their own jobs, had a high level of influence over the senior British manager and could use this to their own advantage.

In the end, he failed to get the full commitment and understanding of the Japanese employees and the company did poorly as a result. The situation improved when head office decided after some years to recall the senior manager and place the younger British manager in charge. With language skills and some experience working in Japanese companies he rapidly changed the organisation, taking into account the above problems and building a more effective rapport with the Japanese employees. He was also able to bring about other improvements through his knowledge of Japanese companies. In particular he changed the head office's approach to the Japanese market and convinced them to invest in building longer-term ties with key clients, rather than focusing on one-off contracts.

A number of British managers were highly critical of Japanese personnel and Japanese management efficiency in general and keen to counter the common view, prevalent in the West, that the Japanese are highly organised and effective managers. In particular it was said that local personnel tended to lack initiative and needed to be spoon-fed with clear and detailed job remits.

Some specific positions and professions carry very different responsibilities in Japan and Western managers must understand these differences if they are to build an effective workforce. The most common difference mentioned by interviewees was with accountants. In Japan accountants tend to have more of a bookkeeping role and play little part in developing financial strategies for companies. Engineers on the other hand tend to have a higher status and a greater involvement in management decisions. This emphasis on technical expertise in Japanese companies was pointed out by a well-known Japanese manager, at the other end of scale in terms of firm size, when Akio Morita made his well-publicised comments about British firms being dominated by accountants and being too financially driven.

Problems between UK HQs and Japan-based operations

Various difficulties, described by both British and Japanese managers in our survey, are related to intra-firm communication and understanding between personnel in the UK and those in Japan. These are hindered by the physical distance between the UK and Japan and by the economic, social and cultural divide that makes the Japanese market so unusual for outsiders. They may also relate to issues of control. Joint-ventures will always involve a degree of power play between the parent companies and several British companies reported significant problems trying to retain an influence over ventures where the most of the staff came from the Japanese parent. Even in subsidiaries, where the most senior manager was Japanese, companies had problems controlling operations from a distance. (One British manager suggested the Japanese often exploit the cultural divide by exaggerating UK-Japan differences and hindering communications to increase their autonomy from UK parent firms).

The commonest complaint coming from representatives in Japan is that they lack support from managers and decision-makers at their HQ. However, we know that tension exists between most subsidiaries and their HQs. The former see local opportunity and push for investment and freedom to follow their own instincts and the latter, balancing the demands of so many divisions and markets, resist and control the allocation of resources across the broader corporate portfolio. But beyond this common problem our findings suggest that Japan is different compared to other major markets. It takes a longer time to fully understand the requirements of the Japanese market and managers and their companies must adapt more significantly to succeed there. Communicating these differences to HQ to enlist the right type of support and bring about the necessary changes in products, services, marketing and general management is a major problem.

The main difficulty lies in getting UK personnel in these various divisions to respond quickly and effectively to Japan's special customer needs. According to our survey one or both of the following two reasons may be the cause:

(1) A lack of importance of the Japanese market financially relative to the firm's other markets.

If Japan accounts for a small proportion of total sales and investment in making required changes may not be warranted by the perceived rewards. However, local managers in Japan will very often suggest that the *lack of investment is the cause* of the limited sales. They argue (and are supported by the data on foreign start-ups in Japan) that long term investment horizons are necessary in Japan. Subsidiary staff also described this as a common general failure in the UK to take the Japanese market seriously, rather than treating it as a minor regional market for existing products.

Having said this it is difficult, when managing at a distance or without first-hand experience, to assess how realistic subsidiary sales forecasts and business expectations actually are.

(2) A lack of understanding about Japan's special requirements, which may result from:
-       too little senior management or board-level experience in Japan
-       poor subsidiary-HQ communications
-       conflicting interests of subsidiary and HQ

-     too little knowledge about HQ objectives or procedures amongst managers in Japan
-     other 'capability' problems such as language or technical skills either at the HQ or the subsidiary.

A number of positive and negative experiences from the survey show how these problems manifest themselves, affect the Japanese operation and can be alleviated.

For a supplier of industrial process equipment for fluid-control a change of management in the subsidiary, from a British expatriate MD to an experienced Japanese President, helped bring about a complete turn-around in the level of commitment and investment it received from the UK HQ. In particular the previous management had failed to understand the special nature of local customer requirements, especially the need to customise products, provide technical support and build long-term ties with larger clients in Japan. The Japanese manager convinced HQ decision-makers that extra investment was needed for the Japan operation to succeed.

Because the subsidiary was a small operator in a large market, contrasting its parent, it required a change of strategy from defending dwindling market share to 'attacking' products brought out by the competition by adding more features. The new manager also initiated changes in subsidiary-HQ communications to improve the responsiveness of UK-staff to product changes prompted by Japanese customers. Convinced of the potential of the Japanese market as a global product leader for specific ranges and the importance of the subsidiary as a future technical service point for other S.E.Asian operations the parent company gave the 'new local administration' full backing.

A British industrial-use ink-jet printer manufacturer, with a subsidiary in Japan and a small team of engineers, steadily increased its local market share. Although Japan only accounted for about 5 percent of its global sales senior managers at the firm's HQ saw Japan as a market leader in terms of learning about product development, customer-led management and manufacturing efficiency. It claimed some success over the past two years, particularly in improving quality levels and customer-responsiveness amongst its production personnel.

The firm's ability to attract more Japanese customers however was limited by the HQ's wish to retain aspects of product innovation and customization in the UK. This was partly influenced by a lack of understanding between affiliate and HQ managers and a perceived conflict of interests. HQ managers had certain fears regarding confidential aspects of new products and existing software technology and Japan-based staff reacted defensively to the lack of trust displayed by their parent (an especially sensitive issue for Japanese employees).

The net effect was that local customers remained dependent on UK-based expertise for some back-up services and product adaptation. At times they were also left unclear as to who was responsible for providing service and repair back-up or customising products and this adversely affected local customer relationships. The Japanese manager of the branch also pointed out that this limited the ability of their office to develop and 'display' technical capabilities which, in this high-tech sector, severely weakened the local reputation of the company in the Japanese market.

The above example recounts a common problem for all foreign firms with overseas branches or affiliates. To fully exploit patents, technical solutions, expertise or strategic information it is often necessary to share it and use around the entire firm, including places where it is some danger of being lost to competitors. There are no general answers, but as regards Japan managers making these difficult decisions should be fully aware of the implications of holding back information as well as the well-highlighted dangers of losing competitive advantages to the Japanese.

For one company the impetus for investing in a local technical centre in Japan came from difficulties the company was having in Japan in the critical areas of sales, maintenance (service) and product customization when carrying some of these functions from a distance. The firm produced precision measuring tools for use at the plant level, which are an important contributor to the quality of output and thus the competitive advantage of the user. The distance between the Japanese customers and the firm's main technical resources in the UK made it difficult for the firm (1) to demonstrate its products and technologies for local marketing purposes; (2) to respond quickly enough to faulty products locally (leaving the subsidiary losing face with the customer), and; (3) to customise products 'on-site' with maximum customer input.

Pushing HQ producers and engineers to adapt products for the Japanese market or provide prompt, reliable service was especially difficult because of the close relationship between UK engineers and UK sales staff, meaning customers in the UK received the best and quickest assistance.

With Japanese sales previously at 25 percent of the group's total, recently fallen to 20 percent, HQ managers were convinced to invest in a local technical centre, primarily for 'local application engineering', or adapting standard equipment into one-off 'specials' products for specific customers.

To assist in this the firm set up a local CAD-CAM design facility connected to its main R&D and production facilities in the UK to provide for a rapid-response back-up for design changes and product adaptations demanded in Japan. This replaced the previous high cost, slow and 'low-intensity' communications previously used which suffered from the lack of local engineering expertise or facilities to 'translate' customer requirements. The company thereby reversed many of the disadvantages listed (1-3) above and provided local technical staff with the resources and motivation, through the display of commitment to its Japan-based operation, to improve the local customer relationships.

Direct clashes in management style were predictably more prominent in joint-ventures and some subsidiaries, where expatriates managed alongside Japanese managers and employees. Very often these organisational problems were initiated or compounded by a lack of understanding from the firm's home base in the UK about the differences and difficulties of Japan. An unstable balance between Western and Japanese management styles or problems over the allocation of decision-making power and control of the enterprise between British and Japanese managers often lay at the heart of these misunderstandings.

Similar misunderstandings affect other aspects of SMEs operations in Japan. The most common set of problems cited by all companies involved in importing products from Britain were to do with the unwillingness or inability of UK producers to adapt their products sufficiently to suit Japanese customers. Comments referred to all aspects of product quality, translation and adaptation of labels and instruction materials, control mechanisms, instrumentation and so on, provision of suitable technical or marketing information and provision of adequate after-sales support.

Managers in branches or subsidiaries in Japan often have too little control over these issues relative to head office personnel, despite being in the best position to assess what adaptations need to be made and why. They are therefore caught between customer demands, which have to be respected if the company is to succeed in Japan, and a lack of commitment, understanding or competence from production units in the UK. In such cases head office must provide the support and facilitate changes at home to back-up the Japan operation if the company is to develop its local presence.

Communication problems often play an important part in creating or exacerbating the various scenarios described above. The SME subsidiary has to effectively convey the special requirements of the Japanese market to head office personnel. Good managers establish an efficient channel of communications with close contacts in various specialist divisions at the UK end to deal with a range of problems at a fairly detailed level. They invest time and effort building their credibility and the commitment of employees at both ends of the connection to implement the necessary changes, not once but continuously. Hence the need to get the best managers involved at the Japan end.

With hindsight some companies realised that good communication channels, that had been developed by 'high flyer' managers responsible for kick-starting the Japanese operation, had deteriorated with the hand-over to a Japanese managing director. As Japanese managers took on more and more decision-making responsibilities at the Japan end this often resulted in weaker and weaker ties with head office functions. In-house understanding of the special needs of the Japanese customer grew significantly but requirements were not transferred effectively to HQ managers or production units because such managers had spent too little (or no) time with the rest of the company. An expatriate representative in Japan as a go-between and, ideally an experienced ex-Japan manager in a senior position at company headquarters, plus frequent visits, secondment programmes and interaction all help alleviate these communications problems.

In one company looked at the Japanese sales people had a similar problem conveying customer requirements back to UK production divisions because they were inexperienced at interacting with Westerners. The weakness of the communications link was found to stem from the subtle, indirect and over-polite way (by British standards) that the Japanese sales managers told production managers in the UK, via faxes or phone calls, what changes were required of various products, packaging or documentation to please customers. The British representative based in Japan eventually had to provide an informal training course instructing them on how to be blunter and more forthcoming in their criticisms and requests!

Finally, it should be noted that very similar problems to the ones listed above affect links between British SMEs in Japan that act as importers and/or distributors for separate companies based in the UK that do not have their own presence. In many cases these problems are accentuated by the fact that the supplier firm's commitment to Japan and knowledge about Japanese customer requirements are even less than in the above cases. British SMEs are often caught in a 'catch-22' situation. On the one hand, with the small volume of shipments and sales in Japan

British exporters have no incentive to adapt products, invest in product promotions or respond efficiently to delivery requests. On the other hand the British sales and distribution SME in Japan cannot increase sales without showing a commitment from UK-based suppliers to respond to customer requirements and build a long-term buyer-supplier relationship.

Difficulties between UK managers and Japanese companies

Many SMEs rely heavily on Japanese companies acting as local representatives in regional markets or in specialist product or sector markets. These firms may be trading companies, distributors, retailers or maintenance and service providers.

As discussed earlier, *experience shows that a company's choice of joint-venture partner, distributor or sales agent when first entering the Japanese market is critical.* They will project the image of the firm and its products directly on to the customer and start building its all-important reputation in the local market. British companies that have succeeded point to the initial 'fit' between themselves and their Japanese partners in terms of their knowledge about the product and its markets, shared business objectives, management style, plus the ability, enthusiasm and commitment to making the product sell successfully in Japan.

Establishing a strong link with a local company can be a frustrating business in Japan, whether you are trying to set up a full-blown joint-venture or a small-scale marketing, sales or distribution agreement. Japanese firms are often very careful from the outset and may require many meetings to build up a rapport with foreign firms. British managers should expect a degree of digging from the Japanese side, into the history and current details of their firm, its status in UK and its strategic strengths, including in particular any special technical competencies it has. These all represent assurances for the Japanese that they are dealing with a trustworthy, well regarded company, before any commitments are made.

Traditionally in Japan the reputation of a firm, and any long-standing informal connections between senior managers, hold much more weight than any legal agreement drawn up between the two parties as the basis for a business partnership. Japanese managers make it a point of principle to know the background, reputation and recognised status of all of their Japanese clients, suppliers, distributors and so on. This often leaves Japanese firms, especially those with little experience beyond their own borders, with something of a dilemma when trying to assess foreign newcomers. Dealing with foreign firms very often makes Japanese managers nervous because they have no basis for judging quality or reliability or the long-term stability of the newcomer. The onus, therefore, is on the foreign company making the initial approach to convey these qualities explicitly.

Similarly the British side must learn about their potential partner's position in the sector networks, *keiretsu* groups and trade associations to 'customise' or tailor the approach and subsequent negotiations. If possible a middleman or mutually-recognised company, agent or consultant should act as the initial go-between and perform introductions. The Japanese dislike 'cold calling' (as we know it) and any prior connection that can assure them of the standing and reputation of the British newcomer will help promote a relationship. Social (or 'socio-business') functions play a very important role in Japanese business and constant 'networking' is required and expected, to get to know potential partners and to get new companies known by those on the lookout for opportunities.

Advice from one British manager suggested that Japanese managers 'feeling out' a prospective foreign business partner will be looking for signs of reliability and stability, that the firm is in Japan for the long-run, that its technical or product attributes are 'genuine'. They are sensitive to the degree of commitment shown by head office personnel and senior management in the UK, and the degree of autonomy afforded the local staff. He advised British firms to *'exude quality at all times, in all interactions'*, including letters, faxes, proposals and advertising and PR materials. Avoid sloppiness at all costs as Japanese managers will see this as a reflection of a lack of standards and quality across all aspects of your business.

A similar message comes across regarding initial face-to-face meetings with prospective Japanese clients, which are the subject of numerous books (of varying quality) on Japanese business etiquette and negotiation tactics (such as Holden and Burgess, 1994; Woronoff, 1991; March, 1990a and 1990b; Maurer, 1989). In a nutshell foreign managers should be polite and respectful, use a softer sales approach, focus on the 'service philosophy' and avoid pushing the 'bottom line' until the Japanese side is ready. Above all *be patient*, avoid looking for immediate decisions and resist forcing the pace of discussions.

This last point results from the tendency for Japanese firms to take a long time making key decisions, particularly those involving doing business with unknown foreign companies. The common counter-tendency is for British (and more-so, American) managers to get impatient or frustrated and either try to push for a decision before the Japanese side is ready, or sometimes to offer a better deal. Both responses can do long-term damage to any business relationship.

Things are, however, changing and British interviewees suggested that the Japanese have recently been speeding up this kind of negotiation process. In the words of one UK manager:

> ...you are likely to get much more out of the first 2 or 3 meetings than ever before, you get into greater detail. Previously these seemed to amount to no

more than casual chats and hard drinking!

For British managers making the initial approach to establish a business relationship there is also often a dilemma over trustworthiness, but it emerges in different ways. It is common, for example, for Japanese trading organisations and distributors to ask for samples of products before signing any formal agreement, in order to assess the product and its potential local market. Where the product incorporated innovative features or advances in technology there was the obvious risk of ideas being copied (a well-known Japanese strength), something made even more likely by the unusual patenting rules in effect in Japan. Not sending material or even requiring a confidentiality clause to be signed before sending samples provides a poor basis for the mutual trust which is essential to these alliances and tends to offend Japanese managers.

Obviously there is no one solution to this and other problems, but British managers must be fully aware of the implications of their actions and the level of interaction that is likely to be expected by Japanese companies. One manager suggested that 'constant attention to the protocol of the relationship was critical from the outset.' This applies in face-to-face meetings and phone or fax contacts throughout the arrangement. Also, make sure there is a healthy exchange of documentation. The Japanese language can be very imprecise, with a large number of ways of saying 'yes' (*hai*), often meaning 'yes I understand' but not meaning 'yes I agree', and very few ways of saying 'no'. As far as possible get all aspects of an agreement written down to clarify what is expected of both sides. Any mis-communication will cause damaging problems later, especially for the foreign partner.

Other problems are to be expected for foreign firms that sell in Japan via distributors, agents or trading companies. This is common amongst SMEs since most cannot afford to by-pass the complex, hierarchical distribution system in Japan the way that Ford or Toys-R-Us can. A major difficulty from the UK-side is that an arms-length relationship does not enable a company's own managers to develop a full understanding of the Japanese market, or develop their own contacts within the relevant corporate networks. The balance between involvement and learning on the UK-side and a degree of autonomy for the Japanese-side is a difficult one to strike.

For many of the companies we have been talking about here, whose products need customising and accompanied by technical support services, poor communications between buyer, middlemen and supplier is a major stumbling block. In some cases distributors or agents can only provide limited technical support and the ideal buyer-supplier relationship described earlier is not possible. Suppliers cannot get specific technical information regarding the types of changes required by customers. Moreover, it is difficult to prioritize customer complaints and demands, that is, to assess which are the most important and warrant investment and which the customer is less concerned about. Hence the market advantage held by large Japanese firms that have both manufacturing and distribution activities.

At the end of the day, in Japan, the *'customer is truly king'*. Buyer outranks supplier in a fundamentally Japanese way. British companies have to completely tailor their initial approach and their on-going relationship with Japanese client companies on this basis. However, as the following section suggests, many of the firms examined for this study derived a range of benefits that went beyond their Japanese operation, from making these changes.

Learning by doing business in Japan

The majority of the managers interviewed, both in Japan and in the UK were highly positive about the benefits of operating in Japan. Many were keen to counter the exaggerated impression that Japanese markets are too tough for British firms. Most of the firms who had been in Japan for some time and had reached a stable level of business activity had, at some stage or another, experienced greater profitability in their Japan operations than elsewhere. Some firms had maintained consistently higher earnings from the beginning. This reflects other figures on foreign companies (of all sizes) in Japan that show they average one percent higher profits than Japanese firms in their own market (described in Chapter 2).

Of course not all firms experience all or even any benefits from venturing into Japan. The problems and costs detailed earlier in this book, plus the numerous stories from interviewees about other firms that had failed to succeed in Japan, attest to the high level of risk. But it certainly worth balancing this negative view with some positive experiences from the UK SMEs we talked to.

Beyond the financial returns there were a range of other benefits gained by companies from their exposure to Japan. These were, in order of importance:

(i)   company-wide improvements in quality levels;
(ii)   product developments led by the Japanese market and technology monitoring activities, and:
(iii) technology transfer to other parts of the firm and to suppliers.

Many of these benefits stem from the changes companies had to make in order to sell products successfully in Japan, which were discussed in Chapter 3 of this book.

Quality improvements

All the firms involved in importing products to Japan and/or manufacturing locally had to adapt products and improve quality levels for the Japanese market. In many cases this provided the motivation and often the direction or benchmark for improving quality levels across many important areas of company activity. This includes the 'quality' of after-sales service, promotional material, technical information, management/manufacturing responsiveness to customer needs and so on, in addition to product quality.

> A senior manager in one of the industrial instruments manufacturers stated that demand for higher levels of quality in the company's Japanese markets had led to corporate-wide changes in quality control, testing and production. The company had adopted a target for 0.1 percent failure rate in products coming off the line which had forced wholesale changes in design, materials testing and on-line checking activities. These changes had in turn altered the firm's purchasing requirements and pushed sub-contractors and suppliers to improve their quality levels. In the 6 months following the change in policy at the company's UK headquarters the company had achieved a 'turn around', averaging 0.5-0.6 percent failure rates across all its sub-components and realised a range of spin-off improvements to other products and down to suppliers.

This is of course the 'ideal' case. Compared to this company the SMEs in general were *far less proactive* and coordinated in their management of such changes and *far more reactive* to the ad-hoc requirements of their Japanese subsidiaries. Benefits were often realised only after a significant amount of pushing from Japan forced UK-based production divisions to adapt to certain customer requirements. These changes then created improvements for other product ranges and enhanced competitiveness in other markets.

Several managers stressed that their UK divisions benefited most from the adoption (to varying degrees) of the Japanese customer-led or customer-first mentality, i.e. *a broad attitude that helped define and improve quality as being what the customer wants rather than what the manufacturer thinks the customer should want.* In one case this was described as a move from using 'commercially acceptable' standards to a mentality of constant improvement. Critically, though, the direction of improvement is dictated first and foremost by the customer, not by technical experts, production managers, product designers or advertising executives who will have their own individual 'benchmarks' from the customer as to what defines quality and functionality. The case-study of the company selling customised wheels to OEMs in Japan, documented earlier (Chapter 3), provides a good illustration of this.

Because of the current stress on 'customerization' and the need for companies to be flexible and responsive to customer requirements in markets everywhere these changes, tailored initially for success in the Japanese market, improved companies' competitiveness elsewhere.

Product development

In many cases products developed for Japan have to be tailored specifically for Japanese customers and are inappropriate for other markets. In other cases, particularly where high-technology products are involved, the Japanese market is ahead of other markets and products in demand here are likely to be wanted elsewhere in time. This was the case for two SME manufacturers selling capital goods (one measuring instruments the other process flow control mechanisms) to Japanese companies. One manager stated that the Japan branch provided the key to the company's broader, global product development strategy. Another described two 'next' generation products which had been produced specifically for the Japanese market and were now sold successfully by the group globally.

Some of the managers interviewed suggested their firms in Japan had a role to 'track' or monitor new technologies and new product ideas as they appeared and feed information back to headquarters. Any firms involved in the consumer electronics sector for instance looked to Japanese markets for the newest product innovations. Similarly, any SMEs subcontracting to the car industry had to keep up-to-date with the requirements of Japanese manufacturers if they were to stay at the leading edge.

Less obvious benefits, which also contributed to corporate competitiveness in general, were derived by some firms through their constant need to develop products for their Japanese sales operations. One illustration of this refers not to the product itself but to the technical manuals and maintenance and service instructions that accompanied the product.

> The local marketing and sales agents taken on by this firm's Japan branch insisted that these were a major weakness of the product package because they were not 'user-friendly' enough. They encouraged the British manufacturer to simplify the instructions, preferably by adding cartoons or illustrations to support technical points in the text (the link with Japanese *'manga'* cartoons was made in the previous chapter). The main reason for this was that the users in this case were more likely to be plant-level operators rather than maintenance engineers, with lower levels of expertise

or specialist training. This reflected the devolvement of responsibility for quality, maintenance and efficiency of production operations to the lowest levels, and the system of employee rotation practised in Japanese manufacturing firms.

One implication of the request was that the British engineers, although highly competent technically, were not focused on the *communications* function of the maintenance documents in terms of the customer requirements. Fulfilling these requirements should be the starting point for any product or part of a product package, rather than being superseded by a display of technical sophistication (VCR manuals tend to fall into the same trap!). This may partly be a reflection of the traditional divide between technical functions (R&D, manufacturing, maintenance etc..) and the 'non-technical' functions (marketing, finance, personnel etc..) that hinders cross-functional organisation in many Western companies.

Convinced that this and other changes were necessary to succeed in Japan, that Japanese customers (corporate or consumers) simply will not accept products in the same way as other customers do, senior managers implemented a programme to encourage a customer-first mentality in (some) other areas of its operations. The value of this organisational change has begun to be reflected in terms of the firm's enhanced competitiveness in its European markets and at home in the UK. In particular the product development requirements of Japanese customers act as a tangible benchmark for reorganisation and improvement.

Many Japanese companies, partly because of their need to constantly respond to customers' demands and partly because of the highly competitive domestic markets in which they evolved, are renown product developers. What they lack in terms of basic R&D skills (less and less in recent years) they make up for in the applied or near-to-market forms of innovation. Large firms like Sony, Canon, NEC and Toshiba in electronics and Toyota, Honda and Mitsubishi in the auto sector are constantly used as benchmarks for Western firms wanting to enhance their ability to commercialise new technologies through customer-led product development (Collinson, 1993 and 1995). But because large Japanese companies are so reliant on networks of smaller sub-contractors for their competitive edge, and because companies of all sizes have to be customer-led to survive in Japan, there are strong indications (though far fewer comprehensive studies) that Japanese SMEs are similarly innovative.

While the kinds of management capabilities that enable a firm to produce new products faster, cheaper and better than its competitors will not automatically 'rub-off' on to foreign SME managers based in Japan, indications from this study suggest that British firms learnt a great deal 'by example'. That is, by being in close proximity to companies that were constantly pushing to develop better products, and by dealing directly with the Japanese managers and engineers that were organising this process, British managers learnt lessons that were helped boost the overall competitiveness of their companies.

Technology transfer

In addition to, or alongside new product technologies some of our companies also transferred manufacturing and processing technologies from Japan to other parts of their firms. In most cases these were passed down to production divisions in the UK or even on to other sub-contractors and suppliers.

An unusual example of this came from a larger SME that was involved in trading activities alongside local manufacturing and adapting imported products. In one project a local Japanese customer required a higher quality of iron casting in the final product and as these components were sourced from an Australian sub-contractor technology known to the final customer (specifically a chemical process to harden the castings) was passed on to them to improve their processing methods. This competitive advantage subsequently proved to be applicable to a wide range of its products, giving the Australian manufacturer a boost in its domestic markets.

There were several similar examples where technology transfer (sometimes licensing agreements) had been initiated by the corporate customer in Japan who wanted to move away from high-cost Japanese suppliers and take on sub-contractors from abroad, while retaining high levels of product quality and reliability.

Some companies were more serious about establishing effective transfer mechanisms than others. Many companies had schemes for engineers, marketing personnel and younger 'high-flyers' to spend short periods based in Japan to learn about customer needs, new technologies and so on and to enhance UK-subsidiary links over the long term. Companies also regularly brought Japanese sales people, engineers and managers to work in the UK to strengthen their understanding of products and production systems and develop closer links with personnel. In addition to the reactive (crisis management) or trouble-shooting trips that had to take place as part of the regular management process the more forward-looking firms set-up these visits with a long-term corporate development strategy in mind.

One of the better SMEs had established a comprehensive management training initiative involving a broader monitoring of 'best practice' in Japan, including visits by Japanese managers to give seminars on Japanese management and marketing. They had also organised training programmes involving an exchange of staff from the firm's Japanese distributor to develop closer ties between production and sales functions.

In an earlier phase of entering the Japanese market this same company had entered into an agreement with one of the largest electronics companies in Japan, as a prelude to a joint-venture to produce and sell a specific product. The initial agreement involved joint development and improvement of production line equipment in preparation for local manufacturing and although full joint-venture plans were scrapped the UK SME learnt a great deal about the Japanese market requirements and new product technologies to help with an independent start-up. Of particular benefit was the way the Japanese parent tied in-house technical expertise closely to customer needs, resulting in a continuous, incremental improvement of products, technical assistance and after-sales service.

Overall then, because Japanese buyers and manufacturers lay such an emphasis on the quality and technical performance of products and sub-components, so must suppliers. Japanese customers will raise issues of quality, reliability and technical efficiency and enter into a close dialogue with their suppliers at the technical level to jointly improve the product. There is far greater buyer involvement than in other markets and the down-side to this is that extra time and extra effort is required. Quick-fix solutions are not acceptable. But considerable benefits also result from these close ties in that the intensive, technically-based interaction provides a detailed stream of information on precisely what the customer really wants in a product or component. This sets a truly customer-led direction for improvements, new designs, features and future product development. At the same time the commitment to meeting buyer expectations is made explicit and a long-term, mutually beneficial relationship is likely to evolve.

Without understanding Japanese buyers, some British companies had the initial attitude that as particular problems with products had not emerged in other markets (where the tendency anyway was to replace faulty parts without investigating the cause of failure) the problem must have resulted from the specific use environment of the buyer. This may be the case, *but to assume so and thereby not investigate customers claims is a fatal mistake in Japan.* In the unlikely event that a foreign firm continues to sell successfully in Japan with this approach they will never derive the potential benefits of close interaction with customers or develop a truly customer-led product development strategy.

Although lessons learnt in Japan have a huge potential to be applied elsewhere, with beneficial effects on overall company performance, most firms did not appear to have a coordinated strategy for learning from Japan. Changes in practices and behaviour at company headquarters, in production divisions or amongst suppliers tended to occur in an ad-hoc manner, only after strong demands were made by senior managers in Japan. 'Knock-on' effects and 'demonstration' effects were important in spreading the benefits when they came to be realised. For instance if the company had to invest in improved promotional material for the Japanese market this would be used by other marketing divisions and subsidiaries. If Japanese customers pushed for certain quality improvements or technical changes and these proved to be economical or attractive to other customers then other division managers would want to adopt them for other markets.

Contrasting the majority, the best of our firms had adopted a *proactive 'learning approach'*, anticipating customer needs and searching in advance for potential problems with products and support services. British managers in these firms stressed the value of using experienced Japanese employees to second-guess customers in this regard. This in turn required an internal office structure and an organisational culture that involved Japanese employees in strategic decision-making.

Overall then, this chapter has examined the main difficulties facing British SMEs in Japan, compared to other overseas markets, and the ways that some of the more successful firms overcame these difficulties. Obviously the lessons vary according to the size, the structure and the sector of the SME in question but there are some general points of value to all firms.

Establishing any sort of presence in Japan is expensive and there can be problems finding the right employees. Market restrictions that act against foreign companies are commonplace, but stem more from the tightly-knit corporate networks ('cooperative competition'), sub-contractor relationships and 'tied' distribution systems than from direct market control by the Japanese government. However, a range of government-related obstacles and bureaucratic hurdles do exist in Japan that foreign firms do not encounter in other overseas markets. Another inherent barrier, until recently, were the preferences of Japanese customers and companies for Japanese-made products. They have long-trusted the quality of local products and relied on the service and support that come with them.

The chapter focused on some of the management (and mis-management) problems experienced by UK SMEs in Japan, which showed how managers coped (or failed to cope) with the above difficulties. Effectively integrating the very different Western and Japanese management cultures, attracting and holding on to experienced Japanese staff, and organising and motivating them when 'owners' and senior decision-makers are directing events from afar is something that successful firms worked hard to achieve. Similarly, dealing directly with Japanese customers, suppliers and competitors, while formulating a management strategy from a distance (in the case of SMEs with UK headquarters) also poses a challenge.

Maintaining the loyalty and enthusiasm of Japanese employees and harnessing their local expertise for the benefit of the company depends on striking the right balance of power between subsidiary and company headquarters. Close monitoring of the subsidiary from UK headquarters is not enough. There needs to be support from managers with Japanese experience in the relevant UK-based divisions, from production to R&D, as well as in senior management. There also needs to be a rich and frequent interaction between home divisions and subsidiary personnel to ensure rapid and accurate response to Japanese client and customer needs. According to the interviewees we spoke to a common fault amongst all foreign firms in Japan was to underestimate or misunderstand the potential management problems and place weak or inappropriate staff in Japan.

Finally, the last section of this chapter looked at how British companies had learned from their experiences in Japan, from supplying demanding consumers and globally-competitive corporate customers in one of the world's toughest markets. Redefining *quality* as something truly customer-driven, enhancing the organisation of product development activities (linking the customer 'front-end' with the rest of the company), and transferring new production technologies from buyer firms are all described in the company case-studies.

5 Conclusions: Costs, benefits and opportunities in Japan

After more than 80 interviews and 30 company case studies examined in the UK and Japan, plus discussions with local experts, government officials and policy makers from both sides, we now know a great deal more about the activities of British SMEs in Japan and the difficulties they face in the Japanese market. The cross-section of SMEs examined provided a range of contrasts across industry sectors, firm sizes and structures, and degree of experience in Japan. Most of the resulting insights are relevant for a wide range of firms with an interest in Japan.

If the overall theme of this book appears to dwell overly on the negative side of Japan and the Japanese, in terms of the problems faced by companies and individual managers, this is only because a comprehensive understanding of these problems is of most practical use to would-be foreign entrants. The British managers we talked to viewed their experience in Japan at the very least as an interesting and enjoyable challenge. Many had clearly developed a *passion* for Japan and a close affinity with Japanese colleagues and friends. They were critical of the Western tendency to exaggerate the negative aspects of the country and its people and to downplay its virtues.

For these managers the costs of entering Japan were outweighed not solely by the personal experience but by the resulting profits and corporate benefits gained. This does not solve the dilemma for would-be entrants considering whether or not to establish themselves in the Japanese market, but knowing what to expect, seeing the problems faced by others and learning the lessons from their experience does help reduce some of the uncertainty. That has been one of the central aims of this book.

Costs and constraints

Experienced managers confirm that there are significant additional costs and constraints associated with the Japanese market that do not exist (or exist to a lesser extent) in other overseas markets where British firms operate. *Japan is different and Japan is difficult.* On the whole these difficulties are more a product of the toughness of the Japanese market and the so-called system of 'cooperative competition' that exists between Japanese firms, rather than 'unfair competition' or 'restrictive practices', although these also exist. For new firms this means a substantially greater investment in time and money is required, compared to other overseas markets, to develop local ties, build a market presence and adapt internal management practices to organise and motivate employees.

The added problems described by British SME managers, and listed in Chapter 4 were:

-       the high basic costs of operating in Japan, including office rents, staff costs (local and expatriates), materials and other inputs;

-       recruitment problems and difficulties keeping good Japanese staff;

-       a range of management problems (within the Japanese operation, with head-office personnel in the UK, and in relationships with local Japanese firms) that result from differences in management style, the unusual requirements of Japanese business practices and customers, and from the cultural differences between Japanese and Westerners;

-       a variety of market restrictions, particularly related to the strong ties between Japanese companies, the activities of trade associations and the convoluted nature of distribution and retail networks, but also a result of the patriotic preferences of Japanese consumers.

-       a range of government-related obstacles, including binding red tape and uncertain regulations pertaining to foreigners and foreign companies.

These closely match the obstacles identified in JETRO's 1995 White Paper on FDI (JETRO, 1995). They rank the 'reported obstacles to the business activities of foreign corporations in Japan' (of all sizes and origins) as follows (from most to least serious):

-       Difficulties in securing manpower

- Competition with Japanese companies
- Strictness of orders from Japanese customers in terms of quality, delivery, etc
- High land costs (rents)
- High costs of labour
- Lack of understanding of overseas head office about Japanese market
- Complexity of distribution system
- Existence of corporate groups
- Government regulations
- Weakness of personal contacts
- Limited decision-making powers in Japan
- Special employment practices of Japan
- Affiliations in distribution

As shown in Chapter 2 and elsewhere, most of these impediments stem from Japan's somewhat unique social, economic and corporate infrastructure which has evolved in the past through the country's relative isolation from the rest of the world and in the rapid growth era following the Second World War. Recruiting experienced, English-speaking Japanese managers, for example, can be difficult because staff tend to remain loyal to their Japanese corporate employers for longer than is common in the West and because companies are loyal to employees and have consistently performed well enough (until very recently) to keep them employed. A continually expanding economy results in low unemployment, low labour mobility and a shortage of available skilled labour. Similarly, business premises were, until recently, extremely expensive in Japan because land is in short supply and city property has been one of the main sectors for investing surplus savings and is used as collateral for corporate bank loans.

Japan has a very different business culture compared to other countries, particularly those in the West (there are more similarities with the emerging Asian economies and arguably with other less developed nations in Latin America and Africa). Personal contact networks and the close-knit, social nature of business relationships mean that foreign firms must adapt their employment practices, their management styles and the way they organise inter-firm linkages to operate in Japan. Moreover, any significant change in business activity in a specific sector, stemming from a new entrant, or even a potential entrant scouting around for opportunities, tends to be noticed. Local firms, distributors, retailers and public-sector agencies are therefore more coordinated and effective in their response, whether this is to accommodate or exclude the newcomer. *As one manager put it: 'if they don't want you to be successful, you won't be'.*

Yet alongside this 'cooperative' business culture amongst networks of

Japanese companies, Japan's domestic markets are extremely competitive, with a high concentration of companies vying intensely for incremental improvements in their local market share. This competitiveness, and the rapid rate of domestic demand-led growth of Japan in the past, have bred perhaps the most discerning customers in the world. To satisfy ever-more stringent consumer demands Japanese companies evolved their focus on quality, manufacturing efficiency, product development and after-sales service and support. These factors then provided the springboard for Japan's corporate competitiveness in international trade, particularly in autos and consumer electronics. The combined system of 'cooperative competition' underlies the development of the *kieretsu* groups, trade associations and the convoluted, partly tied trader-wholesaler-retailer distribution chains in Japan. Again, all of which act as barriers to foreign firms trying to operate in Japan's domestic markets.

The clear indication we gain from experienced foreign managers in Japan is that most of the serious obstacles to market entry into Japan, selling to Japanese customers or corporate buyers, or managing a business in Japan, are all elements that are *intrinsic* to the Japanese economy and deeply ingrained in the national business culture. Contrary to the beliefs of many Western policy makers most are beyond the scope of direct government intervention.

Having identified that these constraints exist, however, *foreign managers are unanimous in their belief that good products sell well in Japan* and UK companies in general are too focused on the difficulties and not on the opportunities of the Japanese market. As one manager put it: "UK firms are reticent about Japan...there is a particular misconception that most foreign firms fail in Japan".

Perhaps worse than this, many firms who do make an attempt to sell in Japan do not take it seriously enough. Without knowing how different Japan is UK firms often send second rate managers and demand quick returns on their investment, using the same benchmarks of success as for other markets. This leads to failure through lack of effort, preparation and adaptability.

Adapting to succeed

The various barriers to entry reviewed above are the source of extra costs for foreign firms investing in a presence in Japan. Once a new company has assessed the costs of office space, local staff, materials, translation costs, the mark-up for sales and distribution and additional service and after-sales support (and the rest), foreign managers must expect to have to wait. If contacts are made, contracts are signed and sales pick up in the first year of operation then a newcomer is unusually lucky. Experience suggests at least three to 4 years 'sitting on the stone', waiting for recognition and the development of reputation, credibility and a sufficient degree of trust for business relationships to begin to evolve and sales to really take off.

By all accounts patience and perseverance are necessary but not sufficient ingredients of success. Various lessons on how to overcome or side-step the barriers to entry into the Japanese market have appeared throughout this book. The most obvious ones are reviewed here.

To begin with, spend time doing your homework, scoping potential markets, creating links, and contacts, assessing the affiliations of the various companies, trade associations, government agencies, distributors and others in your specific sector. Even with a basic understanding of Japanese business practices it should be possible to assess how your market entry is likely to be received by different local alliances and build relationships with this in mind. Contacts and business-related friendships developed behind the scenes are very important.

If possible, bring in a local advisor at an early stage, cultivate links with good lawyers, consultants (even if you have to pay) and particularly with other British managers that have experience in Japan. If the intention is to take on a local Japanese representative president or senior managers, use these contacts to identify and select candidates. Your choice and management of Japanese personnel may well make or break your early attempts in Japan. Senior Japanese managers can provide (or deny) access to relevant sector networks, government bodies and trade associations, as well as customers. They will also play a key role in motivating and organising other Japanese staff, so the balance between local autonomy and an office organised along Japanese lines, versus control from head office in UK and an imposed style of management, must be right.

A champion back in the UK who is knowledgeable and enthusiastic about Japan and committed to investing in opportunities there is a valuable asset. In particular this promotes 'staying power' amongst senior managers that might lose faith if initial sales are slower than in other overseas markets. In several companies we examined this made the difference between early withdrawal and eventual success. A manager with experience of working in Japan can also 'translate' the special requirements of Japanese customers to business operations in the UK and is in a better position to convince them of the need to respond to these requirements quickly and efficiently. In many of the smaller firms it was either the managing director, or at least an influential board member with an interest in, knowledge of and commitment to Japan that pushed for a sustained approach. Maintaining clear lines of communication with head office decision-makers will allow a subsidiary in Japan to meet the needs and wants of local customers most effectively.

Many of the British SMEs showed how poor links with UK-based operations left them prone to many of the problems that affect firms with no local entity in

Japan, limited to exporting from a distance via an agent or distributor. In particular, with poor communications and a lack of direct interaction between key decision-makers and Japanese customers, it can be very difficult to accurately assess and prioritise customer needs. This leaves a firm unable to pinpoint the aspects of quality, the product features or elements of sales and support that might distinguish their product from its rivals. It also means a firm is ill-equipped to adapt products, customise product support services or develop the all-important buyer-supplier relationship and these are key factors for success for foreign firms in Japan.

As shown in Chapters 3 and 4 product customization and development, including appropriate technical brochures (depending on product and sector) and marketing material designed to build a clear image of technical sophistication and quality consciousness are central. More generally Japanese customers will be looking for stability and reliability amongst foreign companies and a long term commitment to support corporate buyers and consumers on-site. The key message is to avoid Western short-termism, the quick-fix, quick turnover, quick profits approach to all aspects of market entry, management, sales and customer relations in Japan. Speed tends not to equate with efficiency, effectiveness, performance or profits. The 'customer *is* king' and any new company, and its product or service development strategy, should be *truly* customer-led.

Of course, there are many foreign firms exporting to Japan via agents, distributors and trading companies, and making good returns doing it. But continued success doing business at 'arms length' from the target market in Japan is only possible in specific product areas. Moreover, it is highly dependent on the efforts, local reputation and quality of the chosen distributor. This leads many exporters, following a period of indirect sales, to establish a presence in Japan, despite the high costs.

Finally, there are obviously an even larger number of SMEs that have adequate sales in their UK or European markets and view the costs of getting into Japan as simply too high. For many the market may be described as 'too big' because of the scale of the changes required in products and packaging and the high costs of product testing, marketing and distribution and of maintaining a Japan-based service and support network. As with any entrepreneurial endeavour, there is obviously no guarantee of success. Much of this book suggests that if you are patient, that if you persevere and continue to invest in Japan, success will come your way. But this message comes from those who have made it in Japan. The failed entrants are not there to be interviewed, so certainly, Japan is not for everyone.

As with all investment decisions involving risk and uncertainty it comes down to belief, belief in the opportunities and likely benefits, tempered by an understanding of the costs, the constraints and the likely problems. However, all the indications from this study and others are that British firms in general believe that Japan's domestic markets are more impenetrable than they really are. *The costs have been exaggerated and the benefits under-emphasised.* If more firms tried, more would succeed in Japan.

Benefits

The validity and importance of the above lessons for newcomers to Japan is underlined by the fact that they come from SME managers who do not have the time, the spare resources or manpower to invest and wait *too long* for success in Japan. Without the finance to buy-in specialist assistance or by-pass the distribution system by using a dedicated in-house sales and delivery force, for example, these firms have had to tackle Japan's special problems head-on. Those that have succeeded have adapted quickly to the above restrictions and shown a clear-cut commitment to their Japanese employees, customers and local counterparts that they are in Japan for the long-term.

Japan offers a range of opportunities for foreign companies, first and foremost because it is such a large, expensive, diversified and sophisticated market, offering the potential to make the highest returns on most good products and services. But also because it is one if the most competitive markets anywhere, representing a tough economic environment in which foreign firms can learn and develop to a high level of international competitiveness. Many of the case studies have shown how improved product technologies, quality and customer service, and the management structures necessarily developed to break into the Japanese market or to remain competitive in Japan have been transferred back to other subsidiaries or the UK headquarters to enhance general corporate competitiveness.

To succeed in Japan requires foreign firms to adapt to its special market requirements, not just at the 'front end' in Japan, but down the line to UK-based operations. Despite the enthusiasm for being customer-led many British firms have not fully implemented this objective beyond the boardrooms and training divisions. Those that have managed to make improvements throughout their companies see this in retrospect as a benefit derived from their exposure to Japan. This learning process does not take place automatically. However, in our study, *reactive* (or 'crisis') management was far more commonplace than *proactive* management, involving forward-looking organisational restructuring on the basis of the requirements of the Japanese market (which was the best route to success in Japan). Companies tended to cope in an ad hoc fashion with the problems thrown up by their operations in Japan, and often only much later found that improvements in products, client responsiveness, customer service or process technologies had improved overall company performance.

Change and opportunity

Most of the firms examined as part of this survey succeeded in entering the Japanese market when it was a tougher place than it is for foreign companies today. *Opportunities for foreign SMEs in Japan are probably better now than ever before.*

Japan has undergone a period of unprecedented change in recent years and the fundamental shifts in its economic, social and political infrastructure are set to continue. Many of these changes are reversible, like prices, costs, exchange rates, economic growth rates everywhere fluctuate and progress in cycles. But many others, at a more fundamental level, are irreversible and have set Japan on a new course into an uncertain future. These changes, described in Chapter 2, have led to significant tensions within the fabric of the Japanese socio-economic framework, in public sector and private sector organisations, and are the source of a new level of concern amongst the Japanese people.

Some observers are heralding a new era, characterised by long-term decline in Japan, in contrast to an accelerated rise in other Asian economies including, in time, China. But this is premature. The current trends point more towards an expansion of economic activity in Asia, with Japan maintaining its position as the regional powerhouse, the largest source of foreign direct investment, and the stepping-stone for access into many of the region's growing markets.

For the most part the current domestic trends point towards a further opening up of Japan and are already advantageous for British companies looking to sell to Japan or establish themselves in Japan's home market. Recessionary pressures mean that Japanese customers and corporate purchasing departments are increasingly concerned about the artificially-high prices of local goods and are increasingly open to imported products. This is part of an irreversible shift away from the traditional, introverted and 'imperfect' domestic market structure and has added considerably to the deterioration of the rigid networks of inter-corporate trading and cross-share-holding amongst Japanese firms that have tended to shut out foreigners.

'*Endaka*', the high-Yen recession was the catalyst for a wide range of changes. Since the mid-1980s the Yen has appreciated by a remarkable amount (up 24 percent from early 1993 to early 1995), making imported products relatively cheaper and more competitive in Japan. Although in US dollar and UK pound-terms the costs of operating in Japan have also risen, real local costs have fallen. Land prices and office rents in particular have declined (some estimates suggest commercial property in Tokyo is 50 percent less in value compared to its peak at the beginning of the 1990s).

Price now matters more in Japan, compared to the past when willingness to adapt products, provide after-sales service and develop long-term customer relationships dominated corporate purchasing decision-making. Japan's distribution system is also changing as competition between retailers and wholesalers grows, discount stores and direct importers provide customers with what they want. Multiple distribution and sales contracts are now possible in many sectors, rather than exclusive agreements and tied sales arrangements.

For foreign companies wishing to establish a permanent presence in Japan other changes make this process easier. In particular, there is now a greater mobility of skilled local labour, with unemployment rising slightly, but many more senior managers now prepared to consider opportunities outside Japanese companies which can no longer guarantee stable and rewarding employment.

Finally, initiatives to promote imports and assist new entrants, established some time ago by the Japanese government (described in Chapter 3), are improving and are becoming better known and better used by foreign firms moving into Japan. At the same time the drive towards deregulation and an opening up of domestic markets in Japan, pushed (and in some cases blocked) for some time at the political level, is having some real effects at the ground-level, improving investment conditions for outsiders. These are somewhat hindered by the tension that has developed in recent years between politicians, bureaucrats and Japanese companies. As the political sphere has dissolved into near-chaos, bureaucrats in the ministries have increased their power over the economy and leading companies have grown more independent of both. The national economic infrastructure that was founded on cooperation between these three organisational pillars is moving into a new, more open and market-driven phase of development.

British government support for SMEs exporting to Japan or looking to establish a base there have also shown a marked improvement in the last 5 years. It would be a mistake for an SME not to enlist the help and experience of these public-sector organisations (reviewed in Chapter 3) in the early stages of their market entry.

Indications of the significant effects of these changes have been appearing for some time. Imports into Japan have in fact been rising in US Dollar terms relative to exports since the mid-1980s, and manufacturing trade has grown from 30 to 58 percent (in 1995) as a proportion of overall imports. Although masked by the appreciation of the Yen and an apparently growing Japanese surplus (until mid-1994), the real balance of trade has been improving for some time. Despite a 10 percent growth of exports from Japan between July 1994 and July 1995, imports into Japan grew by an unprecedented 29 percent, and imports from Europe increased by 34 percent, narrowing the real trade imbalance significantly.

British exports to Japan increased by 35 percent in the first half of 1995, showing that UK firms are quickly taking advantage of the changing market conditions. This indicates the phenomenal degree of change and further emphasises the main message of this book for other British companies that have not taken the plunge into Japan's huge domestic markets. While the lessons from the past are still undoubtedly valid and applicable, British managers must, in the words of one experienced interviewee in Japan, 'lose their old perceptions and take a fresh look at Japan':

The Japanese market is still fast moving, dynamic and difficult. But recession has created a new range of opportunities. Now is open season for new entrants.

Appendix: Useful addresses

In Japan...

British Chamber of Commerce in Japan (BCCJ),
    3F Kenkyusha Eigo Centre Bldg.,
    1-2, Kagurazaka,
    Shinjuku-ku,
    Tokyo 162,
    JAPAN.

    TEL: 03-3267 1901
    FAX: 03-3267 1903

British Embassy Commercial Department,
    No.1 Ichibancho,
    Chiyoda-ku,
    Tokyo 102,
    JAPAN.

    TEL: 03-3265 6340
    FAX: 03-3265 5580

EU-Japan Centre for Industrial Cooperation,
    Nikko Ichibancho Bldg., 4th Floor,
    13-3 Ichibancho,
    Chiyoda-ku, Tokyo 102,
    JAPAN.

TEL: 03-3221 6161
FAX: 03-3221 6226

Foreign Investment in Japan Development Corporation (FIND),
    2nd Floor, Akasaka Twin Tower,
    2-17-22 Akasaka,
    Minato-ku,
    Tokyo 107,
    JAPAN.

    TEL: 03-3224 1203
    FAX: 03-3224 9871

Japan Development Bank,
    International Division,
    9-1 Otemachi 1-chome,
    Chiyoda-ku,
    Tokyo 100,
    JAPAN.

    TEL: 03-3244 1785
    FAX: 03-3245 1938

Japan External Trade Organisation (JETRO),
    Import Promotion Department,
    2-2-5 Toranomon 2-chome,
    Minato-ku, Tokyo 105,
    JAPAN.

    TEL: 03-3582 5511
    FAX: 03-3582 5027

Japanese Chamber of Commerce and Industry,
    3-2-2 Marunouchi,
    Chiyoda-ku,
    Tokyo,
    JAPAN.

In Britain...

Association of British Chambers of Commerce,
    Export Development Officer,
    4, Westwood House,
    Westwood Business Park,
    Coventry, CV4 8HS.

    TEL: 01203-694492

Exports to Japan Unit, Department of Trade and Industry,
    5th Floor, Kingsgate House,
    66-74 Victoria St.,
    London SW1E 6SW.

    TEL: 0171-215 4806
    FAX: 0171-215 2571

Innovation Policy Division, Department of Trade and Industry,
    151 Buckingham Palace Road,
    London SW1W 9SS.

    TEL: 0171-215 1626
    FAX: 0171-215 2909

Japan External Trade Organisation (JETRO),
    Leconfield House,
    Curzon Street,
    London, W1Y 7FB.

    TEL: 0171-493 7226
    FAX: 0171-491 7570

Japan Information Centre,
    9, Grosvenor Square,
    London, W1X 9LB.

    TEL: 0171-493 6030

Japanese Chamber of Commerce and Industry,
    Rooms 493-495, 2nd Floor,
    Salisbury House,
    29, Finsbury Circus,
    London   EC2M 5QQ.

    TEL: 0171-628 0069
    FAX: 0171-629 0248

Japanese Embassy,
    46, Grosvenor Street,
    London, W1X 9LB.

    TEL: 0171-493 6030

Bibliography

Abegglen, J.C. and Stalk Jr., G. (1985), *Kaisha: The Japanese Corporation*, Tuttle publications, Tokyo.

Abrahams, P. (1994), 'Scotch Whisky Producers Take on Tokyo', *Financial Times*, 18.5.94, The Financial Times Limited, London.

Anglo-Japanese Economic Institute (1994), *Britain and Japan 1994/5 - An Economic Briefing*, AJEI, London.

Asahi Shimbun (1995), *Japan Almanac 1995*, Asahi Shimbun Publishing co., Tokyo.

Baker, G. (1995), 'Japanese Land Prices Fall for the 4th Year', *Financial Times*, 20.9.95, The Financial Times Limited, London.

Batchelor, C. (1993), 'A Better Way to Export', *Financial Times*, 5.10.93, The Financial Times Limited, London.

Baxter, A. (1993), 'Construction Equipment Due for a Dig-Out', *Financial Times*, 5.10.93, The Financial Times Limited, London.

Bozell-Gallup (1994), *Bozell-Gallup Worldwide Quality Poll*, Bozell Worldwide, New York.

CEC (1995), *Gateway to Japan: EC Export Promotion Campaign* brochure, European Commission, Brussels.

Collinson, S.C. (1995), 'Organising for Multimedia Product Development: Sony and Philips Compared', *Communications & Strategies*, No.19, pp.47-77, Sept.1995, special issue on 'Technology and Alliance Strategies in Multimedia', IDATE.

Collinson, S.C. (1994), 'A Window of Opportunity,' BCCJ *Insight*, Vol.1, No.4, p.5-8, British Chamber of Commerce in Japan, Tokyo. (The last of a series of three articles by the author).

Collinson, S.C. (1993), 'Managing Product Innovation at Sony: the Development of the Data Discman', *Technology Analysis and Strategic Management*, Vol.5, No.3, pp.285-306, Carfax, Oxford.

Cusumano, M.A. and Nobeoka, K. (1992), 'Structure, Strategy and Performance in Product Development: Observations from the Auto Industry', *Research Policy*, 21, pp.265-293, Elsevier, North-Holland.

Dawkins, W. (1995a), 'Financial Times Survey: Japan in Asia', *Financial Times*,

15.11.95, The Financial Times Limited, London.

Dawkins, W. (1995b), 'Flicker of Light on the Horizon', *Financial Times*, 16.8.95, The Financial Times Limited, London.

Dawkins, W. (1995c), 'Current Account Surplus Down 7.4%', *Financial Times*, 9.11.95, The Financial Times Limited, London.

Dawkins, W. (1994a), 'Loosening of the Corporate Web', *Financial Times*, 30.11.94, The Financial Times Limited, London.

Dawkins, W. (1994b), 'The Return of the High Flyers', *Financial Times*, 6.11.94, The Financial Times Limited, London.

Dawkins, W. and Thomson, R. (1993), 'A Snip at the Tangle of Red Tape', *Financial Times,* 3.9.93, The Financial Times Limited, London.

Donkin, R. (1995), 'Working Out Where to Live', *Financial Times*, 18.8.95, The Financial Times Limited, London.

DTI (1995a), 'Export Promotors', *Japan News*, No.16, Aug.1995, Department of Trade and Industry, DPR Publishing, London.

DTI (1995b), *The British Industry Centre, Japan*, Exports to Japan Unit, Department of Trade and Industry, Heathprint & Associates, London.

DTI (1993), 'Competitiveness', unpublished *Department of Trade and Industry Memorandum*, June, 1993, DTI, London.

Dunne, N. (1994), 'Where the Agreements Came', *Financial Times*, 3.10.94, The Financial Times Limited, London.

Economist (1995), 'Japan's Protection Racket', *The Economist Magazine*, 7.1.95, London.

Economist (1994), 'The Emporia Strike Back', *The Economist Magazine*, 29.10.94, London.

Cortazzi, Sir H. (1993), *Modern Japan: A Concise Survey,* The Japan Times, Macmillan Press, London.

Financial Times (1995a), 'Financial Times Survey: Japan', *Financial Times*, 10.7.95, The Financial Times Limited, London.

Financial Times (1995b), 'Financial Times Survey: Japan in Asia', *Financial Times,* 15.11.95, The Financial Times Limited, London.

Financial Times (1994), 'Financial Times Survey: Japanese Financial Markets', *Financial Times*, 30.3.94, The Financial Times Limited, London.

FIND (1994), *Foreign Investment in Japan Development Corporation Journal,* Vol.2, Winter, 1994, FIND, Tokyo.

FIND (1993), *Foreign Investment in Japan Development Corporation Newsletter*, Nov./Dec. 1993, FIND, Tokyo.

Fisher, A. (1994), 'The End of a Tradition', *Financial Times*, 20.7.94, The Financial Times Limited, London.

Fruin, M. (1992), *The Japanese Enterprise System,* Clarendon Press, Oxford.

Fransman, M. (1995), *Japan's Computer and Communications Industry,* Oxford University Press, Oxford.

Fransman, M. (1992), 'The Japanese Innovation System: How It Works', *Science in Parliament,* Vol.49, No.4, Oct.1992.

Holden, N. and Burgess, M. (1994), *Japanese-led Companies: Understanding How to Make Them Your Customers*, McGraw-Hill, Maidenhead.

Huddlestone Jr., J.N. (1990), *Gaijin Kaisha: Running a Foreign Business in Japan*, Charles E. Tuttle, Tokyo.

Japan Small Business Corporation (1993), *Japan Small Business Corporation (Brochure)*, JSBC, Tokyo.

Japan Times (1994), 'Toy Makers Losing Power to Set Prices', *The Japan Times Newspaper*, 24.3.94, Tokyo.

JETRO (1995), *JETRO White Paper on Foreign Direct Investment 1995*, Japan External Trade Organisation, March 1995, Tokyo.

JETRO (1994a), *Destination Japan: Foreign Investment in Japan: Facts and Figures*, Japan External Trade Organisation, Tokyo.

JETRO (1994b), *Measures for Promoting Foreign Direct Investment in Japan 1994*, Japan External Trade Organisation, Information Service Department, Tokyo.

JETRO (1993a), *JETRO Import Promotion Activities*, Japan External Trade Organisation, Import Promotion Department Progress Report: 1990-1993, Tokyo.

JETRO (1993b), *JETRO Business Support Centre: Your Strategic Base in Japan*, Japan External Trade Organisation, Import Promotion Department brochure, Tokyo.

JETRO London (1995), *JETRO London Update*, Quarterly Briefing from the Japan External Trade Organisation in London.

Keidanren (1993), *Improvement of Business Environment of Foreign Affiliated Companies and the Reform of Japanese Economy*, Dec.21, 1993 (in-house report of the Keidanren).

Lawrence, R.Z. (1992), 'Japan's Low Levels of Inward Investment: The Role of Inhibitions on Acquisitions', *Transnational Corporations*, Vol.1, No.3, pp.47-75.

March, R.M. (1990a), *The Japanese Negotiator*, Kodansha International, London.

March, R.M. (1990b), *The Honourable Customer: Marketing and Selling to the Japanese in the 1990s*, Longman Professional, Melbourne.

Maurer, P.R. (1989), *Competing in Japan*, The Japan Times, Tokyo.

Ministry of Finance statistics and JETRO (1995), *Investment Promotion Fair: Doing Business in Japan*, Japanese External Trade Organisation, Tokyo.

Morimoto, K., (ed.) (1995), *Japan 1995: An International Comparison*, Keizai Koho Center publication, Tokyo.

Nakamoto, M. (1995), 'Signs of Ebbing Strength at Home', *Financial Times*, 1.3.95, The Financial Times Limited, London.

Nakamoto, M. (1994a), 'Bloomin' Bureaucrats', *Financial Times*, 1.7.94, The Financial Times Limited, London.

Nakamoto, M. (1994b), 'Drive into the Rising Sun', *Financial Times*, 17.6.94, The Financial Times Limited, London.

Nakamoto, M. and Abrahams, P. (1994), 'Little Progress in Market Access Discussions', *Financial Times*, 10-2-94, The Financial Times Limited, London.

Owen, J. (1995), 'Working With Industry', *Japan News*, No.16, Aug.1995, Department of Trade and Industry, DPR Publishing, London.

Sazanami, Y. et al. (1995), *Measuring the Costs of Protection in Japan,* Institute for International Economics, Washington DC.

Schlender, B.R. (1994), 'Japan's White Collar Blues', *Fortune Magazine* cover story, 21.3.94.

Sengenberger, W. et al. (eds) (1989), *The Re-Emergence of Small Enterprises: Industrial Restructuring in Industrialisaed Countries,* Institute for Labour Studies, Geneva.

Terazono, E. (1994a), 'Cheap and Cheerful', *Financial Times,* 15.3.94, The Financial Times Limited, London.

Terazono, E. (1994b), 'Hard Road for Japan's Bank Mergers', *Financial Times,* 28.6.94, The Financial Times Limited, London.

Terazono, E. (1994c), 'Imported Beers Boost Market Share in Japan', *Financial Times,* 26.7.94, The Financial Times Limited, London.

Tomkins, R. (1995), 'Japan is World's Favourite Exporter', *Financial Times,* 24.5.95, The Financial Times Limited, London.

Trevor, M. (ed.) (1995), *EU-Japan Business: News from the EU-Japan Centre for Industrial Cooperation,* Vol.8, No.1, 1995, Imageatelier, Tokyo.

Womack, J.P., Jones, D.T. and Roos, D. (1990), *The Machine That Changed the World,* Macmillan, New York.

Woronoff, J. (1991), *The "No-Nonsense" Guide to Doing Business in Japan,* Yohan Publications, Tokyo.